Holdridge Ozro Collins

History of the Illinois National Guard

Holdridge Ozro Collins

History of the Illinois National Guard

ISBN/EAN: 9783337338008

Printed in Europe, USA, Canada, Australia, Japan

Cover: Foto ©ninafisch / pixelio.de

More available books at **www.hansebooks.com**

HISTORY

ILLINOIS NATIONAL GUARD,

FROM THE

ORGANIZATION OF THE FIRST REGIMENT,
IN SEPTEMBER, 1874,

TO THE

ENACTMENT OF THE MILITARY CODE,
IN MAY, 1879.

⟶⟵

By

HOLDRIDGE O. COLLINS,
Late Lieutenant Colonel and Assistant Adjutant-General.

⟶⟵

"Et quorum pars *parva* fui."

⟶⟵

CHICAGO:
PRESS OF BLACK & BEACH, 170 S. CLARK ST.
1884.

Nostra Turbimur Epsi.

Holdridge Ozro Collins.

Preface.

"Little shall I grace my cause
In speaking for myself. Yet, by your gracious patience,
I will a round unvarnish'd tale deliver."

THE Organization of the Illinois National
Guard, in 1875, was the result of a long-
growing conviction that the State must have
a Militia, well trained and equipped, which
could be relied upon with confidence in emergencies.

The necessity for such a force was more
apparent in the large cities and populous
communities, where the civil authorities needed a power-
ful aid to check lawlessness and disorder.

The reaction in regard to Military matters after the
war, had caused an almost total neglect of the Militia in
Illinois; but the occasional rumblings of a disturbing
element had been heard in various localities, more especially in Chicago, and the citizens of this city were
finally aroused to a realization of the fact that it was

entirely without any safeguards, other than the police
force, and that a general riot would throw the entire
community into the hands of the lawless.

In 1874, by the aid of individual subscriptions, six
companies of volunteers were enlisted, uniformed, armed
and commissioned as the First Regiment. This was the
nucleus of the large force organized into a Brigade in 1875
and 1876, that gave the State, almost at a bound, a
Military Service which compared favorably with the
Militia of the Sister States.

An attempt has been made in the following pages to
give an account of this movement, and the legislation
growing out of it.

Perhaps the story of the First Regiment has been
dwelt upon longer than necessary, but the great influence exercised by its officers and men in hastening the
consolidation of Regiments and Battalions throughout the
State, and the pride of the writer, as one of the earliest
members of that body, in its present standing, the First
in discipline and drill as well as in name, may excuse
what otherwise might have been an uninteresting statement of trivial particulars.

The author may be pardoned in speaking of himself
sufficiently to show the sources of his information in the
compilation of the following pages.

He was a member of the National Guard, with the
exception of three months in the Spring of 1875, from
the formation of the First Regiment, in September, 1874,
until June, 1879, the period covered by this book. During that time, he held all the ranks, from private to
Lieutenant-Colonel, in the First Regiment, and on the

Brigade and Division Staff. As Assistant Adjutant-General of the Brigade and Division, the entire official correspondence passed through his hands, and the original of all letters received, and copies of all orders and communications transmitted, were carefully preserved. The statements made herein are from the records, and, it is confidently believed, in accordance with the facts.

It was the intention originally to refer but very briefly to the enactment of the peculiar law of 1879, but since these pages were commenced, gentlemen, prominent in the Militia, have thought that the interests of the service, as well as justice to all who were defeated in their attempts to secure a good law by the Thirty-first General Assembly, required the story. The writer has made no allegations for which he is not responsible. He has overdrawn nothing, " nor set down aught in malice." On the contrary, should the accuracy of that narrative be questioned, records, documents and letters can be produced showing that the half has not been told.

Bearing in mind Solomon's statement, " of making many books there is no end," and Job's warning, " Oh! that mine adversary had written a book," the author hopes that this history may prove of some interest to the many gentlemen with whom he enjoyed four years of pleasant Military association.

HOLDRIDGE O. COLLINS.

CHICAGO, February 22, 1884.

I.

The Organization of the First Regiment.

THE First meeting to effect the organization of a Regiment of Militia was held in Chicago, at the Grand Pacific Hotel on August 28, 1874. Subsequent meetings were had in the early part of September, at the Sherman House and the Tremont House, and there being an unanimous feeling for immediate action, a general outline of the mode of procedure was speedily agreed upon, the minordetails being left for future consideration.

Guerdon S. Hubbard, Jr., very generously offered his building, Nos. 79 and 81 State street, without compensation, for the use of the Regiment, until definite arrangements could be made for an Armory, and the next meeting was held at that place, on September 8, where Companies A, B and C were enrolled.

The following was their respective membership:

COMPANY A.

Captain, - - - -	Graeme Stewart.
First Lieutenant, - - -	Julius G. Goodrich.
Second Lieutenant, - - -	Charles S. Diehl.
First Sergeant, - - -	R. W. Rathborne.
Second Sergeant, - - -	N. N. Goodrich.
Third Sergeant, - - -	George Miles.
Fourth Sergeant, - - -	John McArthur, Jr.

PRIVATES.

A. W. Merriam, J. C. King, E. R. Richards, John M. Dandy, Charles H. Smith, Chas. Jernegan, Chas. Rand, A. Bushey, E. R. Chumasero, H. F. Boynton, Saml. Brown, W. S. Carpenter, C. M. Bickford, Geo. M. Hough, J. W. Street, C. Barry, E. W. Westfall, E. Mead, G. P. Bartalott, Geo. Cane, L. F. Wade, F. Dodge, C. H. Besley, C. S. Wells, E. S. Magill, W. G. Sherer, John Vaughn, C. Pettet, John S. Clark, D. Smith, M. A. Farr, W. W. Powell, O. Huyck, G. H. Corneles, A. L. Chatterton, H. Brainerd, A. J. Hugeman, O. H. Secrest, F. Larger, C. McArthur, P. R. Woodford, Will. Chambers. Will. Creighton.

COMPANY B.

Captain, - - - -	Edwin B. Knox.
First Lieutenant, - - - -	W. W. Bishop.
Second Lieutenant, - - -	Arthur J. Howe.

PRIVATES.

John Brine, W. H. Brine, W. H. Lane, W. D. Gregory, S. C. Goodyear, W. H. Baldwin, C. N. Bishop, F. E. Fenderson, C. W. Butler, F. K. Morrell, E. Archibald, Miles Burnam, E. E. Russell, Frank Reed, Saml. Sheahan, Henry S. Bowler, Charles W. Cutting, F. C. Lovejoy, Will. Rathbone, E. Durand, W. L. Prettyman, Charles E. Case, E W Thomas, D. J. Foley,

Rodney Granger, C. W. Parker, S. W. Stryker, J. E. Muchmore, Jr., S. P. Anderson, G. H. Stevens, J. Dermott, W. Booth, S. Smith, C. W. Hornick, J. T. Hoyne, F. Guth, George Dickson, George Coombs, F. H. Sharp, O. H. Beedy, D. J. Kennedy, C. D. Thompson, C. S. Dunk.

COMPANY C.

Captain,   -   -   -   Mason B. Carpenter.
First Lieutenant, -   -   -   Irving R. Fisher.
Second Lieutenant, -   -   -   Noble B. Judah.
First Sergeant,   -   -   -   -   John D. Bangs.
Second Sergeant,   -   -   Holdridge O. Collins.

PRIVATES.

J. Y. Oliver, J. W. Johnson, George A. Gibbs, C. H. Hubbard, Henry J. Peet, Henry W. Seman, A. W. Brickwood, B. M. Saunders, W. P. Conger, W. D. McCool, C. F. Hamilton, J. C. Clark, Francis O. Lyman, Azel F. Hatch, Harry C. Gorin, Saml. F. McConnell, Leonard Boyce, Edwin O. Brown, W. L. Johnson, B. W. Dodson, N. B. Brant, D. W. Graves, E. Hanecy, W. E. Mason, W. E. Cooke, J. H. Shields, Warren L. Ayers, George Hough, H. R. Vanderwont, Josiah Johnson, Frank G. Hoyne, H. S. Freeman, J. H. Starkweather, Fred. S. Wheaton, G. E. Pomeroy, A. O. Lindsley, C. H. Hill, E. W. Jamar, F. W. Sanger, Wm. Schatz, W. H. Peek, J. W. Montgomery, Fred. Mills, J. W. Hawley, P. Cook, George Cook, O. O. Hall, C. V. Coon.

These three Companies reporting at the same meeting, the rank of their Captains was decided by lot, Captain Stewart winning the right of the line, Captain Knox the left and Captain Carpenter the colors.

On September 14th, Company D was received into the Regiment. It was composed of the following gentlemen:

Captain,	-	-	-	-	John W. Hawley.
First Lieutenant,		-	-	-	Wm. Dickinson.
Second Lieutenant,	-		-	-	C. H. Spellman.

PRIVATES.

Parsons Cooke, C. C. Chase, Frank Ray, J. W. Dickinson, Charles Mathas, W. Garnet, John Woodbridge, Jr., J. H. Elliott, Charles D. Blaney, George Corwith, Philip Larrabee, E. J. Webster, Wm. Burrell, J. Richards, H. Carter H. Spellman, Richard Holmes, John Wilson, R. Hobson, W. G. Tucker, Herbert Dennington, F. Marshall, Charles Stewart, L. Williams, E. Tehle, J. R. Blaney.

The necessity for a Field officer being apparent, by the unanimous voice of the entire command, Gen. Frank T. Sherman was elected Major of the Battalion.

The enthusiasm with which these four companies had been enlisted, and the material assistance promised by the Governor of the State and many liberal citizens of Chicago, indicated the permanent success of this movement, and several independent Militia companies in Chicago made application to be received into the Regiment.

As their tenders of service were accompanied, however, with the demands that they be accepted with their individual uniform, and take rank in the Regiment according to the date of their Captains' commissions, etc., etc., it was not thought expedient to receive any old commissioned company, and the following preamble and resolutions were adopted.

" WHEREAS, It is desirous that the Regiment be filled with ten acceptable Companies ; Therefore, be it

" *Resolved*, 1st, That no company of men shall be admitted to this Regimental organization, unless the company or body of men shall be recruited by recruiting officers regularly appointed by the Battalion Commander; 2d, That recruiting officers be appointed by the Battalion Commander, to recruit the remaining companies to complete the Regiment."

In accordance with the foregoing, Messrs. C. A. Bishop, A. W. Merriam and Holdridge O. Collins were appointed recruiting officers.

The uncertainty and confusion arising from the attempt to arrange the minute affairs of the organization in " committee of the whole," showed the necessity for standing and special Committees, and the following were elected:

Order of Business—Capt. M. B. Carpenter, Lieut. I. R. Fisher, Fred. K. Morrill, S. P. Anderson, F. B. Reed.

Ways and Means—Capt. Graeme Stewart, Capt. E. B. Knox, H. J. Goodrich, D. J. Kennedy, Capt. M. B. Carpenter.

Rules of Order—J. H. Haynie, Capt. John W. Hawley, W. D. Gregory, W. H. Lane, Sergeant Holdridge O. Collins.

At a business meeting, held Monday evening, October 5th, and presided over by Major Sherman, two new companies, E, with 43 men, and F, with 41 men, were presented by regularly appointed recruiting officers, and received into the Regiment.

Their officers were as follows:

COMPANY E.

Captain, - - -	Holdridge O. Collins.
First Lieutenant, - - -	Samuel Appleton.
Second " - - -	Gilbert M. Holmes.

COMPANY F.

Captain, - - - -	William Black.
First Lieutenant, - - -	Wm. P. Gunthorp.
Second " - - -	H. F. Boynton.

By the organization of the last two companies, the Battalion became entitled to a Lieutenant Colonel, and Major Sherman was promoted to that office without a dissenting voice; Guerdon S. Hubbard, Jr., was elected to the vacant Majority. Lieut. Chas. S. Diehl was detailed as Adjutant, and he filled this position to the satisfaction of the entire command until the Staff was completed by regular appointments. No member of the Regiment worked harder for its success than Lieut. Diehl. Identified with it from its inception, he enlisted as a private, and was elected from the ranks Second Lieutenant, upon the organization of Company A. He devoted much time and severe labor in the early days, and by his personal exertions he raised many hundreds of dollars to equip the Regiment and place it on an independent basis. He remained with the command up to 1883, when he resigned as Lieutenant Colonel, having been promoted to that rank through all the lower grades.

The first Staff of the Regiment appointed by Col. Sherman was composed of the following gentlemen:

Adjutant, - - First Lieutenant James H. Haynie.
Quartermaster, - First Lieutenant Charles H. Gillespie.
Surgeon, - - - Major Ben. C. Miller, M. D.
First Assistant Surgeon, - Captain Henry Hooper, M. D.
Second " " First Lieutenant E. W. Sawyer, M. D.
Chaplain, - - - - Captain David Swing.

The six companies immediately commenced drilling, and the large attendance and prompt obedience to their instructors soon brought about a more Military aspect of affairs and a regular system of discipline.

It was not contemplated in the beginning of this
movement that members should pay the cost of their
uniform and equipments. In the absence of any law by
which funds could be drawn from the State Treasury,
assurances had been given that a sufficient amount of
money could be raised from the citizens of Chicago, by
voluntary subscription, to uniform the Regiment and pay
a portion of its current expenses. It now became necessary to call upon the City to do its share of the work.

The officers of the Citizens' Association of Chicago were
requested to inspect the Battalion and present its necessities to the public in an authorized form.

On October 26th, Gen. A. L. Chetlain, Gen. A. C.
McClurg and Mr. J. C. Ambler, a committee from the
Citizens' Association, reviewed the Regiment and en-
quired into its wants. Their report to the Association
was voluminous and highly laudatory and concluded as
follows:

" From our observation and inspection, and from what we
can gather in reply to our enquiries, we do not hesitate to
report that the material composing the First Regiment Illinois
State Guard, is excellent, both physically and morally, in the
military acceptation of that word, and that there is an evidence
of quiet, determined ambition to excel as citizen soldiers, of
willingness to undergo the ordeals of drill and discipline, that
cannot fail,if proper encouragement be given them, to make them
into a good and serviceable Regiment, worthy of the sympathy
and support of our citizens, and we cordially recommend them
to your favorable consideration and that of the Community at
large."

Upon the request of the Regiment, the Citizens' Association appointed an Auditing Committee or Board, for

the " equipment fund " of the Regiment, composed of
Gen. A. L. Chetlain, Walter Kimball, C. B. Nelson, Gen.
A. C. McClurg and R. P. Derrickson, gentlemen well
known by the community, and whose names were a
guaranty that the money of the Regiment would be properly expended.

The Regiment thereupon appointed a committee of
eighteen to solicit subscriptions. Said committee was
composed of the officers of the six companies, viz:

Graeme Stewart,   -   Captain Company A.
J. G. Goodrich,   -   -   First Lieutenant Company A.
Chas. S. Diehl,   -   Second Lieutenant Company A.
Edwin B. Knox, -   -   Captain Company B.
W. W. Bishop,   -   - First Lieutenant Company B.
Arthur J. Howe, -   -   Second Lieutenant Company B.
Mason B. Carpenter, - - Captain Company C.
Irving R. Fisher, -   -   First Lieutenant Company C.
John D. Bangs,   -   - Second Lieutenant Company C.
John W. Hawley, -   - Captain Company D.
J. W. Dickinson,   -   - First Lieutenant Company D.
Walter G. Goodrich,   -   Second Lieutenant Company D.
Holdridge O. Collins,   - Captain Company E.
Samuel Appleton, -   - First Lieutenant Company E.
Geo. McDonald,   -   - Second Lieutenant Company E.
William Black,   -   - Captain Company F.
W. P. Gunthorp,   -   - First Lieutenant Company F.
H. F. Boynton,   -   - Second Lieutenant Company F.

Under the direction and supervision of this committee
of officers, the entire Regiment was divided into squads
of zealous canvassers, and armed with the recommendation of the Citizens' Association and their blank subscription list, they commenced their labors.

These proceedings had fully prepared the public for the attack upon its purse, and all classes of citizens responded liberally to the call, from Geo. M. Pullman who started the list with $500, followed by twenty-two gentlemen, each of whom subscribed $100, down to the " Connecticut pie man " with his no less generous donation of five dollars. The labor of canvassing so large a city and visiting all of the more prominent citizens was great, and consumed much time, and taxed to the utmost the energies and patience of those who had the matter in charge. It would perhaps be invidious to make any comparisons where all did so well, but the success accompanying the unusual exertions of Captain Stewart and Lieut. Diehl of Company A, Captain Knox of Company B, Captain Carpenter and Lieut. Bangs of Company C, Captain Black of Company F, and Color Sergeant Bell of Company E, deserves especial recognition. A sufficient fund was raised by this personal solicitation of members of the Regiment to warrant the renting of a permanent Armory and to purchase the uniform.

Commodious quarters at No. 112 Lake street were selected and the Regiment entered into possession and commenced an earnest and severe course of drill and instruction. The gray uniform of the First Regiment Infantry of the Connecticut National Guard was adopted, and Messrs. Stryker & Co. of New York City, contracted to deliver the entire outfit by May, 1875.

Article IV of the Code of " Rules and Regulations of the First Regiment Illinois State Guard," adopted September 21, 1874, provided as follows:

" ELECTIONS.

" All elections for field and line officers shall be by ballot, and shall take place annually, on the first Tuesday in December."

Pursuant to the foregoing, on December 1, 1874, the regular annual meeting was held, and officers for the ensuing year were elected. Gen. Sherman declined a reelection, as he was unable to devote the attention to the Regiment necessarily required by its Commander.

The following gentlemen were chosen:

Lieutenant Colonel,	Alexander C. McClurg.
Major,	Guerdon S. Hubbard, Jr.

COMPANY A.

Captain,	A. M. Ferris.
First Lieutenant,	Chas. Jernegan.
Second "	Chas. S. Diehl.

COMPANY B.

Captain,	Edwin B. Knox.
First Lieutenant,	W. W. Bishop.
Second "	Henry S. Bowler.

COMPANY C.

Captain,	Mason B. Carpenter.
First Lieutenant,	Frank B. Davis.
Second "	John D. Bangs.

COMPANY D.

Captain,	John W. Hawley.
First Lieutenant,	Wm. Dickinson.
Second "	F. P. Dix.

COMPANY E.

Captain,	Holdridge O. Collins.
First Lieutenant,	Samuel Appleton.
Second "	Gilbert M. Holmes.

COMPANY F.

Captain,	William Black.
First Lieutenant,	Robert B. Lewis.
Second "	Wm. P. Gunthorp.

At this meeting a new Company, formerly known as the Ellsworth Zouaves, was added to the Regiment, and given the letter G. Its officers were:

Captain,	Edward S. Whitehead.
First Lieutenant,	Henry B. Maxwell.
Second "	John H. Johnson.

By direction of Governor Beveridge, the Adjutant General of the State, Col. A. L. Higgins, made a requisition upon the General Government for arms, and on January 14, 1875, the first invoice arrived from the United States Armory, at Springfield, Mass., and was turned over to Quartermaster Gillespie.

Regimental order No. 10, in February, 1875, announced Col. McClurg's Staff, as follows:

Adjutant,	First Lieutenant Benjamin W. Underwood.
Quartermaster,	" " Charles H. Gillespie.
Surgeon,	Major Charles G. Smith, M. D.
Assistant Surgeon,	Capt. Henry Hooper, M. D.
Chaplain,	Capt. David Swing.

On March 13, 1875, a new Company, commanded by

Captain,	-	-	-	-	E. T. Sawyer.
First Lieutenant,		-	-	-	E. Norton.
Second "		-	-	-	Geo. H. Bohner.

was enrolled and given the letter H.

The Regiment, now having eight Companies; became entitled to the full complement of Field and Staff, and the following gentlemen were elected and commissioned as the Field Officers:

Colonel,	-	-	-	Alexander C. McClurg.
Lieutenant Colonel,		-	-	Guerdon S. Hubbard, Jr.
Major,	-	-	-	-	Edwin B. Knox.

In February, 1875, riotous demonstrations in Chicago were made, directed more especially against the treasury and building of the Relief and Aid Society. The prompt assembling of the First Regiment, and the knowledge that its six Companies were bivouacked in its Armory, ready to sally forth at a moment's notice, fully armed and equipped, probably had a greater effect than any other cause in preventing an outbreak of the communistic element at that time. The Chicago papers were prompt in recognizing the Regiment as one of the most material aids in saving the city from the threatened violence. And there was generally manifested by the public a feeling of satisfaction over the formation of so finely a disciplined force of Militia.

In March, steps were taken to secure the passage of a new Militia law by the Legislature, but the lateness of the Session, and above all the differences of opinion as to the most desirable provisions of a new military code, prevented any concerted action, and the Legislature adjourned without amending the old, unsatisfactory Militia law, much to the regret of those who had taken an interest in a Militia reörganization throughout the State.

At a business meeting of the Regiment, held May 29, 1875, the Committee on Ways and Means reported that the

Amount subscribed by citizens towards the equipment fund was	-	-	-	$13,468 50
Paid by members of the Regiment		-		2,349 50
Total	-	-	-	$15,818 00

All of which was being properly expended for uniforms and equipments, under the direction of the Auditing Board.

A new company of 35 men was admitted. It was given the letter I, and its officers were:

Captain,	-	-	-	-	-	J. Scoville.
First Lieutenant,		-	-	-	John H. Burns.
Second "		-	-	-	W. E. Hall.

Subsequently Company K was admitted, completing the ten companies of the Regiment. The first officers of Company K were:

Captain,	-	-	-	Charles W. Daniels.
First Lieutenant,		-	-	T. L. Clarke.
Second "		-	-	Charles W. Deane.

In the spring of 1875, Mrs. Jesse Whitehead pressed into the military service a band of young ladies, and their generosity, taste and skill had provided a beautiful stand of colors, which Gen. J. D. Webster, on their behalf, presented to the Regiment, on the morning of May 13, at the Exposition building.

The Regiment appeared on the streets of Chicago,

in uniform, for the first time, the same day (May 13, 1875), when it acted as escort to the Grand Army of the Republic, at its annual meeting. The first public parade, however, for the purpose of being formally received by the Executive of the State, took place on July 28, 1875, at South Park. Companies A, B, C, D, E and F, only, were represented in line. The Command was reviewed by Gov. Beveridge, Lieut. Gen. P. H. Sheridan, of the Army, and Brig. Gen. A. C. Ducat, commanding Illinois National Guard.

So great interest had been manifested, and curiosity had been so highly raised, that a large number of spectators was present to see in what manner the promises made by the Regiment had been fulfilled. That the public expectations were not disappointed appears from the Chicago papers in their notices of this review, and Harper's Weekly of August 21, 1875, containing an illustration of the parade, used the following language:

"This Regiment shows a perfection in drill, marching and military carriage that is truly surprising, and gives evidence that very many of the line officers as well as the field have seen service. It is to-day as great a favorite in Chicago as the "Seventh" is in New York, for, like the last-named Regiment, it is composed of men of high standing, whose great aim is to excel. At its first parade, it was enthusiastically received by the citizens and distinguished visitors from abroad, and from Gen. Sheridan and other military men received high commendation."

At the annual meeting, Tuesday, December 7, 1875, Col. McClurg declined a reëlection, and Lieut. Col. Hubbard refused to accept a well-earned promotion. Capt. George R. Davis, of Company A, was elected Colonel,

Lieut Col. Hubbard and Maj. Knox being severally reëlected. In the spring of 1876, Maj. Knox resigned his commission, and on May 24th, Samuel B. Sherer was elected to the vacant office. Lieut. Col. Hubbard also resigned in the summer, and Col. Davis, having been elected in November a member of the House of Representatives in Congress, from the Second District, was likewise compelled to sever his connection with the Regiment.

At the next annual meeting, held December 5, 1876, Maj. Sherer, the only field officer of the Regiment, was unanimously elected Lieutenant Colonel, which office he held until his resignation, in August, 1877, when Maj. Swain assumed command, Col. McClurg being at this time in Europe. Lieut. Col. Sherer commanded the Regiment during the riots of July, 1877, and his services were prompt and efficient. Gov. Cullom realized that the State could illy afford at this time to lose so valuable an officer, and he was immediately commissioned Colonel of the First Regiment of Cavalry. His exertions soon gave that body an efficient organization, and he was thereupon promoted to the rank of Brigadier General and Chief of Cavalry of the State, upon the Staff of the Governor.

The First Regiment owes its present existence to the three gentlemen, Col. McClurg, Lieut. Col. Hubbard and Major Knox. In the dark days of 1874 and 1875 when so many despaired of success, and officers and men dropped out so rapidly that the complexion of entire companies was changed in a few months, and it seemed as if the movement must be abandoned, these gentlemen by their "*fortiter in re*"

represented by Col. McClurg and Major Knox. and

"*Suaviter in modo,*"

of which Col. Hubbard was the exponent, kept the Regiment together. Their courage and cheerfulness, and their labors in procuring money by voluntary donation from the public, at a time of almost unexampled pecuniary distress in the history of the Country, are deserving of all praise. Major Knox was and is now an officer of the regular Army upon the retired list, with rank of First Lieutenant, and he is the best tactician the Regiment has had. On October 15, 1877, he was elected Captain of Company F, and was induced to renew his connection with the Regiment. He was again elected Major, July 30, 1878, upon the resignation of Major A. L. Goldsmith; Lieutenant Colonel, March 19, 1879, to fill the vacancy caused by the resignation of Lieut. Col. Williams, and upon the promotion of Colonel Fitz-Simons as Brigadier General of the First Brigade, Lieut. Col. Knox was unanimously elected Colonel, October 31, 1882, which office he now holds.

Colonel McClurg and Lieut. Col. Hubbard both served with high rank in the late war of the Rebellion, and their ripe expereince and high social position fitted them to be the organizers and leaders of this movement, and carry it on to success. Lieut. Col. Hubbard was the first man in Chicago to come forward with something besides *advice* for the help of the Regiment. The definite *materialization* of the command took place in the building which Col. Hubbard had gratuitously presented for its use, as has been heretofore intimated. He accepted the Majority very reluctantly, and only from a sense of duty. He was very popular in the Regiment, and nothing but his decided refusal to accept the office, prevented his election as Colonel, in December, 1875.

That Col. McClurg's efforts were fully appreciated is shown from the circumstance of his having been speedily called upon to resume the command. He was suffered to remain in retirement but a short time, and notwithstanding his reluctance, on March 12, 1877, he was again placed at the head of the Regiment, which position he held until his resignation, in November, 1877.

On March 12, 1877, Edgar D. Swain was elected Major, and at this date the field officers were:

Colonel, - - -	Alexander C. McClurg.
Lieutenant Colonel. - - -	Samuel B. Sherer.
Major, - - - -	Edgar D. Swain

Lieut. Col. Sherer resigned August 28, 1877, and Major Swain was elected his successor, Alfred L. Goldsmith, Captain of Company D, being promoted to the Majority. Major Goldsmith resigned July 1, 1878, and on July 30, Edwin B. Knox, Captain of Company F, was elected to this vacancy, as above stated.

Upon the resignation of Col. McClurg in 1877, Lieut. Col. Swain became Colonel, and Rudolph Williams, Captain of Company G, was elected Lieutenant Colonel. In January, 1878 the field officers were :

Colonel, - - - -	Edgar D. Swain.
Lieutenant Colonel, - -	Rudolph Williams.
Major, - - - - -	Alfred L. Goldsmith.

Immediately after assuming command as Major, Col. Swain realized that the Regiment could have no independent and assured existence for the future, unless it secured a building of its own, properly planned and erected for military uses, and he turned his attention to this object. The Regiment had been particularly fortunate in having for its Commanding Officers gentlemen of ability and determination, but the erection of an Armory had heretofore appeared to them all, too great an undertaking, without aid from the State. In March, 1876, an unsuccessful effort had been made to to secure an appropriation from the City Council, for the renting of an Armory. Col. Swain vowed that the Regiment should have its own Armory — and the Armory was erected. Ground was broken on the site of old Trinity Church, April 18, 1878, and on May 18, 1878, as the Commander of the Regiment, in the presence of the Civic officers of Chicago, the entire military force of Cook County, commanded by its Brigadier General, and acting as escort to the Major General, with the assistance of the Grand Lodge A. F. & A. M. of Illinois, Col. Swain had the proud satisfaction of laying the Corner Stone of the very commodious and picturesque building on Jackson street, which his patience, energy and determination had secured. The Armory was formally dedicated October 29, 1878, by appropriate ceremonies, and the Regiment has had a local habitation, as well as a name, since that time. Col. Swain resigned in October, 1881, greatly to the regret of his comrades, and he is now one of the most popular officers of the Veteran Corps.

Col. Swain was succeeded by Col. Charles Fitz-Simons, who was promoted, in October, 1882, as Brigadier General of the First Brigade.

Upon the promotion of Major Knox as Lieutenant Colonel, in March, 1879, J. Henry Truman was elected Major, and upon his resignation in the following December, John D. Bangs was rewarded for his long and faithful services as Quartermaster by being elected to the vacant Majority. After the resignation of Major Bangs, Capt. Diehl was promoted to the Majority, and when Lieut. Col. Knox became Colonel, upon the promotion of Col. Fitz-Simons, Major Diehl was the choice of the Regiment for the vacant Lieutenant Colonelcy, and Henry S. Bowler, Captain of Company B, became Major. He succeeded as Lieutenant Colonel upon the resignation of Lieut. Col. Diehl, in 1883, Wm. L. Lindsay, Captain of Company G, becoming Major. The present Field Officers of the Regiment are:

Edwin B. Knox, Colonel.

Henry S. Bowler, Lieutenant Colonel.

Wm. L. Lindsay, Major.

The changes in the Field and Line officers have been very rapid, owing to the cosmopolitan character of Chicago. Col. Knox is now the only one of the original officers who has an active connection with the Regiment, and even his service has not been continuous.

For the benefit of the curious and those having a personal interest in the history of the Regiment, a table is subjoined, showing the names of the first officers of the ten companies *who were commissioned*, and of all of the field officers, down to the present time:

LINE.

COMPANY A.

Date of Commission.

Captain,	A. M. Ferris,	December 1, 1874.
First Lieutenant,	Chas. Jernegan,	" " "
Second Lieutenant,	Chas. S. Diehl,	September 8, 1874.

COMPANY B.

Captain,	Edwin B. Knox,	September 8, 1874.
First Lieutenant,	W. W. Bishop,	" " "
Second Lieutenant,	Henry S. Bowler,	" " "

COMPANY C.

Captain,	Mason B. Carpenter,	September 8, 1874.
First Lieutenant,	Frank B. Davis,	December 1, 1874.
Second Lieutenant,	John D. Bangs,	September 8, 1874.

COMPANY D.

Captain,	John W. Hawley,	September 15, 1874.
First Lieutenant,	Wm. Dickinson,	" " "
Second Lieutenant,	Frank A. Dix,	December 1, 1874.

COMPANY E.

Captain,	Holdridge O. Collins,	September 16, 1874.
First Lieutenant,	Samuel Appleton,	" " "
Second Lieutenant,	Gilbert M. Holmes,	" " "

COMPANY F.

Captain,	William Black,	September 28, 1874.
First Lieutenant,	Robert B. Lewis,	December 1, 1874.
Second Lieutenant,	Wm. P. Gunthorp,	" " "

COMPANY G.

Captain,	Edward S. Whitehead,	December 1, 1874.
First Lieutenant,	Henry B. Maxwell,	" " "
Second Lieutenant,	John H. Johnson,	" " "

COMPANY H.

Captain,	E. T. Sawyer,	March 13, 1875.
First Lieutenant,	E. Norton,	" " "
Second Lieutenant,	Geo. H. Bohner,	April 20, 1875.

COMPANY I.

Captain,	C. R. E. Koch,	May	29, 1875.
First Lieutenant,	Chas. A. Starkweather,	"	" "
Second Lieutenant,	Garrett M. Vanzwoll,	"	" "

COMPANY K.

Captain,	Charles W. Daniels,	September	15, 1875.
First Lieutenant,	T. L. Clarke,	"	" "
Second Lieutenant	Charles W. Dean,	"	" "

FIELD.

	ELECTED.	PROMOTED.	RESIGNED.
Majors :			
Frank T. Sherman.....	September 14, 1874	October 5, 1874	
Guerdon S. Hubbard, Jr.	October 5, 1874	April 3, 1875	
Edwin B. Knox........	April 10, 1875		Feb. 14, 1876.
Samuel B. Sherer......	May 24, 1876	December 5, 1876	
Edgar D. Swain........	March 12, 1877	August 28, 1877	
Alfred L. Goldsmith...	August 28, 1877		July 1, 1878.
Edwin B. Knox........	July 30, 1878	March 19, 1879	
J. Henry Truman	April 17, 1879		Dec. 1, 1879.
John D. Bangs.........	January 5, 1880		Jan. 1, 1882.
Charles S. Diehl	March 26, 1882	October 31, 1882	
Henry S. Bowler.......	October 31, 1882	August 8, 1883	
Wm. L. Lindsay.......	August 8, 1883		
Lieutenant Colonels :			
Frank T. Sherman.....	October 5, 1874		Dec. 1, 1874.
Alexander C. McClurg.	December 1, 1874	March 13, 1875	
Guerdon S. Hubbard. Jr	April 3, 1875		Sept. 1, 1876.
Samuel B. Sherer	December 5, 1876		Aug. 28, 1877.
Edgar D. Swain	August 28, 1877	December 1, 1877	
Rudolph Williams.....	December 1, 1877		Feb. 1, 1879.
Edwin B. Knox	March 19, 1879	October 31, 1882	
Charles S. Diehl	October 31, 1882		April 16, 1883.
Henry S. Bowler.......	August 8, 1883		
Colonels :			
Alexander C. McClurg.	March 13, 1875		Dec. 7, 1875.
George R. Davis.......	December 7, 1875		Nov. 21, 1876.
Alexander C. McClurg.	March 12, 1877		Nov. 13, 1877.
Edgar D. Swain	December 1, 1877		Oct. 31, 1881.
Charles Fitz-Simons....	February 20, 1882	October 20, 1882	
Edwin B. Knox........	October 31, 1882		

II.

The Formation of Regiments and Battalions throughout the State.

THE Favorable reception of a Regiment of Militia in Chicago was an incentive for the organization of other similar bodies in the more populous Counties of the State, and very soon, enrolments of many independent Companies were reported to the Adjutant General, with requisitions for arms and requests for assignment.

The following Companies were commissioned in rapid succession:

COMPANY.	LOCATION.	CAPTAIN.	DATE.
Harris Guards..............	Petersburg	Cornelius Rorke.......	October 8, 1874.
Altona Rifles	Altona	William Whiting......	October 19, 1874.
Belleville Guards	Belleville	Cassimer Andel........	November 14, 1874.
Morris Guards	Morris.....	Robert B. Horrie	December 10, 1874.
Livingston County Guards.	Pontiac	John Hudson (Lieut.)...	January 13, 1875.
Sherman Guards	Pawnee.........	Dwight M. Hamlin	January 25, 1875.
Nokomis Guards	Nokomis	John Carstens	February 10, 1875.
Washington Guards	Belvidere	M. J. Flynn............	March 23, 1875.
Moline Rifles	Moline	L. S. Rasmussen.......	April 20, 1875.
Watseka Rifles	Watseka	Mathew H. Peters......	May 19, 1875.
National Blues	Peoria.........	John Hough...........	June 4, 1875.
Cullom Guards	Williamsville ..	William C. Gilbreath...	June 14, 1875.
Elmira Guards............	Elmira.....	David Jackson (Lieut.),.	July 3, 1875.
Union Guards	Sycamore	R. A. Smith...........	July 21, 1875.
Bohemian Rifles	Chicago.........	Prokop Hudek	August 9, 1875.
Veteran Guards...........	Peoria.........	Thomas Cosgrove......	August 11, 1875.
Franklin Guards..........	Benton.	John H. Hogan	August 14, 1875.
Streator Guards...........	Streator........	C. W. Keller	August 17, 1875.
Fairfield Guards..........	Fairfield	John R. Handly........	August 19, 1875.
Atlanta Light-Guards	Atlanta	Ira A. Church.........	August 23, 1875.
Pana Guards	Pana	John Handly	September 13, 1875.
Marion Guards............	Marion.........	James V. Grider........	September 20, 1875.
Sycamore Guards.........	Sycamore.......	W. W. Wharry	September 21, 1875.
Keokuk Junction Guards...	Keokuk Junct..	C. E. Hennick...........	October 27, 1875.
Lincoln Guards...........	Quincy	Samuel Bynum...........	October 30, 1875.

COMPANY.	LOCATION.	CAPTAIN.	DATE.
Emmet Guards	Peoria	Thomas Lynch	December 6, 1875.
Galva Guards	Galva	N. Flansburg	December 30, 1875.
Company A, 2d Regiment	Chicago	E. J. Cunniff	December 7, 1875.
Company B, 2d Regiment	Chicago	P. J. O'Connor	December 7, 1875.
Company C, 2d Regiment	Chicago	Thomas Meaney	February 1, 1876.
Company D, 2d Regiment	Chicago	Joe A. Eagle	December 7, 1875.
Company E, 2d Regiment	Chicago	Daniel Quirk	December 7, 1875.
Company F, 2d Regiment	Chicago	I. H. Donlon	March 13, 1876.
Company G, 2d Regiment	Chicago	M. J. Dooley	January 18, 1876.
Company H, 2d Regiment	Chicago	Wm. G. Marsh	March 1, 1876.
Shelby County Guards	Cowden	Cass Burrus	January 17, 1876.
Bowensburg Guards	Bowensburg	A. E. McNeal	January 17, 1876.
Veteran Guards	Streator	George W. Landes	January 25, 1876.
Oneida Guards	Oneida	Orrin P. Cooley	January 27, 1876.
Carthage Blues	Carthage	Chas. A. Gilchrist	January 28, 1876.
Pontiac Guards	Pontiac	H. B. Reed	January 29, 1876.
Sterling Guards	Sterling	Wm. R. Adams	January 31, 1876.
Kewanee Guards	Kewanee	John Butterinck	February 6, 1876.
Marseilles Guards	Marseilles	J. W. Preston	February 9, 1876.
Creston Guards	Creston	J. C. Sprigg	February 12, 1876.
Williams County Guards	Crab Orchard	Jas. Cunningham	February 16, 1876.
Danville Guards	Danville	Amos S. Cowan	February 22, 1876.
Aurora Light-Guards	Aurora	J. M. Vosburg	March 6, 1876.
La Salle Light-Guards	La Salle	Wm. Aitkin	March 16, 1876.
DANVILLE BATTERY	Danville	Edmund Winter	March 17, 1876.
Piper City Guards	Piper City	H. C. Baughman	March 21, 1876.
Chicago Light Cavalry	Chicago	Geo. M. Miller	March 30, 1876.
Logan Guards	Murpheysboro	Gill J. Burr	April 13, 1876.
Westfall Zouaves	Bushnell	C. C. Morse	May 1, 1876.
Hilliard Guards	Wataga	E. L. Thomas	May 12, 1876.
Quincy National Guards	Quincy	Elisha B. Hamilton	May 15, 1876.
Sherman Guards	Springfield	Benjamin F. Spangler	May 20, 1876.
Joliet Citizens' Corps	Joliet	Daniel C. Hayes	May 23, 1876.
Naperville Guards	Naperville	J. F. Strokechen	May 27, 1876.
Wyoming Light-Guards	Wyoming	H. J. Cosgrove	June 1, 1876.
Paris Guards	Paris	Joseph W. Vance	June 7, 1876.
Glenn Rifles	Mt. Sterling	N. S. Westbrook	June 14, 1876.
Taylorville Guards	Taylorville	Wm. T. Vandever	June 19, 1876.
Astoria Guards	Astoria	Charles Wilson	June 20, 1876.
Odell Guards	Odell	J. K. Howard	June 27, 1876.
Quincy Veterans	Quincy	Francis Aid (Lieut.)	July 1, 1876.
Rockford Guards	Rockford	C. M. Brazee	July 22, 1876.
Morgan County Guards	Jacksonville	James M. Swales	July 25, 1876.
St. Clair Guards	East St. Louis	Willis E. Finch	July 28, 1876.
Morgan Cadets	Jacksonville	Wm. Harrison	August 1, 1876.
Galena Guards	Galena	Wm. Pittam	August 4, 1876.
Governor's Guards	Springfield	James E. Hill (Lieut.)	August 14, 1876.
Dwight Guards	Dwight	S. H. Kenney	August 26, 1876.
Augusta Guards	Augusta	Ell. Gillett	September 1, 1876.
Homer Light-Guards	Homer	Geo. W. Caines	September, 30, 1876.

The eight new Companies of Infantry in Chicago, consolidated into the Second Regiment, were composed of Irish-American citizens, and their organization was modeled after the famous Sixty-Ninth Regiment of New York. They labored under considerable discouragement at first, but owing to the indefatigable exertions of Brig. Gen. Ducat, James Quirk, its first Commander, William J. Onahan, John J. Healy, Thomas Brennan, Thomas Hoyne and other zealous gentlemen, who had at heart the formation of an Irish Regiment in Chicago, all obstacles were surmounted; uniforms were purchased, an armory was obtained, and the State supplied the arms and equipments. The following gentlemen composed the original Field and Staff:

James Quirk, Lieutenant Colonel.

John Murphy, Major.

Wm. P. Dunne, Major and Surgeon.

John Lanigan, First Lieutenant and Adjutant.

Wm. J. Onahan, First Lieutenant and Quartermaster.

During the Railroad riots of 1877 in Chicago, the Second Regiment was stationed in the most dangerous portion of the city, and its prompt suppression of disorder, and steady obedience to its superior officers, gained for it the good wishes and thanks of the citizens, as well as a national reputation. The following telegram was read to the Regiment when drawn up in line at the Halsted street viaduct, on the morning of July 28, 1877:

" HEADQUARTERS 69TH REGIMENT, N. Y. S. M.

NEW YORK CITY, July 27, 1877.

Lieut. Col. James Quirk:

" In the name of the 69th and other Irish-American Regi-

ments, I congratulate the Second Regiment of Illinois Militia
on doing their duty by the Country in this eventful crisis.

" JAMES CAVANAGH,

" *Colonel Commanding.*"

Gov. John L. Beveridge devoted much personal attention to the reorganization of the State Militia. An
old campaigner himself, he was well qualified by his experience to assume the duties, as well as the rank of
Commander-in-Chief of the State forces. In the early part
of 1875, he realized that he was working at great disadvan-
tage by reason of the numerous reports, requisitions and requests made to him directly from the numerous unassigned Companies, and that the proper expedition of
these matters demanded the appointment of an intermediate commanding officer, who would relieve him of the
tedious detail of the organization by condensing reports
and accounts, and making general and special recommendations.

Section 3 of the Militia Law then in force, entitled
" An Act to revise the law in relation to the State
Militia," approved March 23, 1874, practically gave him
the right to appoint as many Major and Brigadier Generals as he thought proper, but he determined to commence by placing the entire force under the command of
one Brigadier General.

Illinois embraced among her citizens many gentlemen who had been greatly distinguished in the late war
for their executive ability and military skill and acumen
in the command of the Brigade, Division and Corps, and
the Governor was not at a loss to find material suitable
for his purpose.

His choice fell upon Gen. Arthur C. Ducat, of Chicago, a gentleman whose military experience, rank and services in the War of the Rebellion, eminently fitted him for the arduous duties of such a command.

Gen. Ducat enlisted as a private in the Twelfth Illinois Infantry, in May, 1861. He was rapidly promoted, and in April, 1862, he became Lieutenant Colonel of the same regiment. He served as Chief of Staff of Maj. Gen. E. O. C. Ord and Maj. Gen. William S. Rosecrans, and in November, 1862, he was assigned by the President as Inspector General of the Army of the Cumberland, under Maj. Gen. George H. Thomas. In consequence of physical disabilities acquired in the service, he resigned from the army in 1864, with the rank of Brevet Brigadier General.

His discharge bears the following autograph endorsement, an unusual honor:

" HEADQUARTERS MIL. DIV. OF THE MISS.,
" NASHVILLE, Tenn., Feb. 19, 1864.
" Lieut. Col. Ducat leaves the service in consequence of ill health alone. His services have been valuable, and fully appreciated by all those under whom he has served, as is shown by the fact that he rose from the position of a private, then First Lieutenant and Adjutant of his Regiment, to the Lieutenant Colonel of it, and finally Assistant Inspector General of the Department of the Cumberland.
" U. S. GRANT, *Maj. Gen.*"

Gen. Ducat accepted the command of the Illinois National Guard with great reluctance, knowing well the difficulties of the undertaking. The term " military discipline " was not at that time very clearly defined in the minds of the Militia, and some of the first measures of the

General, which were of a radical and positive character, caused so many protests and objections, that on August 10, 1875, he tendered his resignation. Gov. Beveridge, however, wisely refused to accept it, and calling his attention to paragraph 4 of General Order No. 1, under date of August 1, 1875, viz., " The General commanding will take such measures, under the law, *as in his judgment he deems proper*, for the discipline, inspection and efficiency of the troops under his command," gave him the emphatic promise that his course should receive the hearty support of the Executive.

With such an assurance of confidence, Gen. Ducat felt himself under obligations to proceed, and he entered upon the work, determined to carry through his measures of reform, discipline and organization, regardless of the consequences to individuals or commands. How well that work was done, and how firmly he was sustained by Gov. Beveridge during the remainder of his administration, this record will show.

In July, 1875, a change was made in the office of Adjutant General of the State, by the appointment of Col. H. Hilliard. Col. Hilliard was an old soldier, having seen service on many battlefields. He had executive abilities of high order, and he was entirely competent to assume the duties of Adjutant and Quartermaster General of the State. Soon after his appointment, at a personal interview in Chicago, Gen. Ducat gave him a general outline of his plan of organization, and he did afford very material assistance to the Governor and Gen. Ducat in their efforts to consolidate and discipline the rapidly augmenting forces.

Pursuant to the plan of Gen. Ducat, immediate steps were taken to assign the Companies to Regiments or Battalions, and by December, 1876, the following consolidations had been effected:

FIRST REGIMENT.

Organized at Chicago; Col. George R. Davis, commanding.

SECOND REGIMEMT.

Organized at Chicago; Lieut. Col. James Quirk, commanding.

THIRD REGIMENT.

Sycamore Union Guards.

Sycamore Guards.

Sterling Guards.

Creston Guards.

Aurora Light-Guards.

LaSalle Light-Guards.

Naperville Guards.

Rockford Guards.

Galena Guards.

Chicago Bohemian Rifles.

The first election of Field Officers was held on January 15, 1876, at La Salle, and resulted in the choice of the following gentlemen:

Colonel, J. W. R. Stambaugh, Captain of Sterling Guards.

Lieutenant Colonel, John B. Day, of La Salle.

Major, L. C. Mills, of Streator.

The first Adjutant was Lieut. S. S. Auchmoedy, of Sterling.

Fourth Regiment.

Altona Rifles.

Peoria National Blues.

Peoria Veteran Guards.

Peoria Emmet Guards.

Elmira Guards.

Galva Guards.

Oneida Guards.

Kewanee Guards.

Wataga Hilliard Guards.

Wyoming Light-Guards.

The first Field Officers were elected at Peoria, on February 2, 1876, viz:

Colonel, John Hough, Captain Peoria National Blues.

Lieutenant Colonel, Wm. Whiting, Captain Altona Rifles.

Major, A. T. Johnson, Captain Kewanee Guards.

Lieut. James Welsh, of Peoria, was appointed the first Adjutant.

Fifth Regiment.

Petersburg Harris Guards.

Nokomis Guards.

Williamsville Cullom Guards.

Atlanta Light-Guards.

Cowden Shelby County Guards.

Springfield Sherman Guards.

Springfield Governor's Guards.

Taylorville Guards.

Jacksonville Morgan County Guards.

Jacksonville Morgan Cadets.

The original Field Officers were:

Colonel, John A. Howard, of Pana.

Lieutenant Colonel, Ira A. Church, Captain Atlanta Light-Guards.

Major, Louis H. Williams, of Cowden.

The first Adjutant was Lieut. W. Jordon, of Pana.

SIXTH REGIMENT.

Students of the State Industrial School at Champaign, forming Companies A, B, C, D, E, F, G and H, Colonel Edward Snyder comanding.

SEVENTH BATTALION.

Belleville Guards.

Benton Franklin Guards.

Fairfield Guards.

Marion Guards.

Crainville Guards.

Capt. J. W. Landrum of the Crainville Guards, being the Senior Officer, was directed to assume command of the Battalion. This consolidation was but temporary, and soon after the Governor made a different assignment of the Companies.

EIGHTH REGIMENT.

Moline Rifles.

Keokuk Junction Guards.

Quincy Lincoln Guards.

Quincy National Guards.

Quincy Veteran Guards.

Bowensberg Guards.

Carthage Blues.

Bushnell Westfall Zouaves.

Mt. Sterling Glen Rifles.

Astoria Guards.

Augusta Guards.

This Regiment was organized at Peoria, on February 2, 1876, by the election of the following gentlemen as Field Officers:

Colonel, Wm. Hanna, Captain Keokuk Junction Guards.

Lieutenant Colonel, E. K. Westfall, Captain Bushnell Westfall Zouaves.

Major, R. R. McMullen, Captain Quincy Veterans.

Lieut. C. Hennick, of Keokuk Junction, was appointed the first Adjutant.

NINTH BATTALION.

Watseka Rifles.

Danville Guards.

DANVILLE BATTERY.

Piper City Guards.

Paris Light-Guards.

Homer Light-Guards.

The first Commander was W. H. Chandler, elected Major on April 6, 1876, at Danville.

Lieut. J. E. Field, of Danville, was the first Adjutant.

TENTH BATTALION.

Streator Guards.

Pontiac Guards.

Marseilles Guards.

Joliet Citizens' Corps.

Odell Guards.

Dwight Guards.

The first election of Field Officers, held at Dwight on August 16, 1876, placed the following gentlemen in command:

Lieutenant Colonel, J. B. Parsons, Captain Dwight Guards.

Major, L. C. Mills, Captain Streator Guards.

Lieut. John B. Fithian, of Joliet, was appointed the first Adjutant.

In his Biennial report for the years 1875 and 1876, Adjutant General Hilliard, showed clearly the rapid progress made, and demonstrated an unmistakable desire throughout the State for a thorougly equipped and disciplined Militia. His recommendations were based upon a perfect knowledge of the requirements of the service and zeal for its improvement. He refers to Gen. Ducat and the Field and Staff, as follows (*Vide* pp. 10, 11):

"I desire here to say that great praise is due to Brig. Gen. Arthur C. Ducat, and his staff officers, for the able and efficient manner in which they have performed their duties. This department is largely indebted to these gentlemen for their able assistance and generous advice. As a body composed largely of veterans who have seen service, they will rank with a like number of military officials of our sister States. The Field and Staff officers, also, of the Battalions as organized, have evinced, in the main, a desire to bring their commands up to a high state of discipline, and great praise is due to them for the great personal sacrifices they have made to advance the interests of the State troops."

The term of Gov. Beveridge expired Monday, January 8, 1877, when he was succeeded by Gov. Shelby M. Cullom. In his message to the Thirtieth General Assembly, Gov. Beveridge used the following language, in referring to the Militia:

" An unusual interest in military affairs, for a time of peace, has of late been manifested throughout the State. The Adjutant General has been very active and effective in organizing and arming the Militia. July 1, 1875, the total organized military force in the State was 895 men and officers, consisting of one Regiment of eight companies and twelve detached companies. September 30, 1876, the total force was 5,146, constituting a Brigade of seven Regiments, three Battalions and eight detached companies, aggregating eighty-five companies.

" All these organizations are independent and voluntary, and can disband at pleasure. The members give their time and, with such aid as can be obtained from citizens, furnish their own uniform and armories. The State supplies the arms. There is no term of enlistment. The men merely sign a muster roll; they take no oath; they assume no obligation, except what a sense of military pride may impose, and there is no power to enforce obedience. The officers elected are commissioned by the Governor, and any refusal of officer or men to obey the orders of the Commander-in-Chief can only be remedied by revoking the commission, disbanding the company and calling in the arms.

" Such a military system is valueless in war, and its only value in peace is in the pride of the men and the honor of the citizens who voluntarily form these independent organizations.

" The Militia Law of the State is very crude and imperfect, and needs revision. In my opinion, the state should provide for the organization and discipline of a limited number of Regiments, and for the encouragement of such organization and the preservation of its own property, should provide, at least, suitable armories. A well-organized Militia, composed of our own citizens, will not endanger the liberties of the people, but on the contrary, give greater security to life, property and liberty."

The foregoing statement demonstrated the very defective condition of the State Militia Law, and the great obstacles which had been surmounted to achieve so gratifying a success.

Gov. Beveridge refers in very flattering terms to his Adjutant General, and too modestly refrains from any statement of his own labors; but the great interest he took in the Militia, almost from the day of his inauguration; the encouragement and promise of aid given by him both as an official and private citizen; his many journeys to different parts of the State, for the purpose of personally superintending the enrolment of Companies and consolidation of Regiments and Battalions, and his prompt and effective requisitions upon the General Government for arms and equipments, are too generally known to need comment.

Governor Cullom fully appreciated the necessity for a reliable, armed citizen soldiery, and in his Inaugural Message to the Thirtieth General Assembly, he referred to the subject in the following concise and emphatic terms:

" I desire to add one suggestion in reference to the affairs of our own State, by calling your attention to the Militia Law. I believe a more perfect law should be enacted, which will secure a more thorough organization of the State Militia.

" The spirit of our institutions, and the temper of our people, are hostile to a standing army ; and I am opposed to any policy, State or National, looking to governing the people by the bayonet. Yet, in the most highly-civilized communities, a trained Militia, recruited from the intelligent and industrious classes, is an almost indispensable auxiliary to the civil power, in the interests of peace and good order."

III.

The Brigade and the Militia Law of 1877.

ARTHUR C. DUCAT was appointed Brigadier General, June 8, 1875, and General Order No. 1, directing him to assume command of all the Military forces of the State of Illinois, and appoint a Staff, was issued from Springfield, dated August 1, 1875.

General Order No. 3, bearing date, Springfield, December 21, 1875, consolidating the forces into Regiments and Battalions, as shown in the preceding chapter, was issued simultaneously with Gen. Ducat's first order, under the same date, from Brigade Headquarters at Chicago, assuming the command.

The following gentlemen were announced as the Brigade Staff:

E. A. Otis, Colonel and Chief of Staff, Chicago.

Geo. I. Waterman, Lt. Col. and Asst. Adjt. Gen., Chicago.

Wm. E. Strong, Lt. Col. and Inspector Gen. Chicago.

Francis Morgan, Lt. Col. and Chf. of Artillery, Chicago.

Albert L. Coe, Major and Quartermaster, Chicago.

G. S. Dana, Major and Commissary, Springfield.

Ben. C. Miller, Major and Surgeon, Chicago.

Isaac Poole, Captain and Assistant Surgeon, Evanston.

P. W. Plank, Capt. and Asst. Inspector, Champaign.

J. M. Hosford, Capt. and Asst. Inspector, Genesseo.

Noble B. Wiggins, Capt. and Asst. Insp., Springfield.

A. L. Whitehall, Capt. and Asst. Inspector, Watseka.

H. E. Selby, Capt. and Asst. Insp., Keokuk Junction.

J. K. Howard, Capt. and Assistant Inspector, Odell.

Henry B. Ayers, Capt. and Asst. Inspector, Peoria.

Henry B. Maxwell, Capt. and Asst. Insp., Chicago.

John Hawley, First Lieut. and Aide-de-Camp, Chicago.

Henry B. Whitehouse, First Lt. and Aide-de-Camp, Chicago.

Holdridge O. Collins, First Lieut. and Aide-de-Camp, Chicago.

Nearly all of these officers had been distinguished for services in the late war, and their intelligent coöperation soon placed their several departments in a very creditable condition of efficiency. Gen. Strong entered the United States service in May, 1861, as Captain of Company F, Second Wisconsin Infantry, and in November, 1864, he became Lieutenant Colonel of the Twelfth Wisconsin Infantry. He served during the war as Inspector General Right Wing, Army of the Tennessee, under Major Gen. James B. McPherson; as Inspector General of the Seventeenth Army Corps, and as Inspector General of the Department and Army of the Tennessee, retaining this latter position till after the close of the war. He was Inspector General of the " Freedman's Bureau," from May, 1865, to September, 1866, when he was mustered out, with the rank of Brevet Brigadier General.

The sudden and exacting demands upon the Quartermaster's Department during the riots of July, 1877, found Major Coe fully prepared for all emergencies, and the very full and complete inspection records of Gen. Strong, pointed out almost to a man the forces which could be relied upon for effective duty.

The several commands were so widely scattered that a large number of Assistant Inspecting Officers were required, and these were appointed as they became necessary throughout the State.

On August 25, 1876, Gen. Strong issued, in the form of General Order No. 2, from the Brigade Headquarters, full instructions for a thorough inspection of the entire Militia, and his orders were, in the main, carried out by the Assistant Inspectors. His consolidated report was the first document of the kind filed in the Adjutant General's office since the close of the war, and was considered of so much interest and importance that it was set out at large in the Biennial Report of the Adjutant General for 1875 and 1876. (*Vide* pp. 23–43.)

During the summer and autumn of 1876, Gen. Ducat made many visits throughout the State, for the purpose of inspecting and reviewing the different local commands, and he was everywhere received with enthusiasm, and encouraged to persevere in a course of thorough discipline. He met with an universal desire for a Militia law which would afford a revenue sufficient to pay for the actual necessities of the service, and a sanction for the enforcement of discipline, and he was urged to prepare a Bill for the next Legislature.

Acceding to these wishes, Commanding officers of Regiments and Battalions were requested to send him memoranda of their wants and suggestions in regard to the proposed new law; and a copy of the following was sent to all commands in the State.

" CHICAGO. Nov. 25, 1876.

"CIRCULAR NO. 1.

" The following officers are appointed a Commission to frame a Military Code for the State of Illinois, to be submitted to the consideration of the next Legislature, to wit:

Col. E. A. Otis, Chief of Staff, Chicago.

Col. John Hough, 4th Regt. Inf., Peoria, Ills.

Col. J. W. R. Stambaugh, 3 Regt. Inf., Sterling, Ills.

Col. W. D. Richardson, 5th   "   "

Col. J. T. Torrence,   2d   "   "   Chicago.

Lt. Col. W. E. Strong, Inspector General, Chicago.

Lt. Col. Geo. I. Waterman, Asst. Adjt. Genl., Chicago.

Lt. Col. Francis Morgan, Chief of Artillery, Chicago.

Lt. Col. James Quirk, 2d Regt. Inf., Chicago.

Capt. Geo. M. Miller, 1st Regt. Light Cav., Chicago.

Capt. Jas. M. DeWitt, 1st   "   Infty.,   "

Capt. F. B. Davis,   1st Regt. Infty.,   "

Capt. Chas. Jernegan, 1st Regt. Infty.,   "

Lieut. H. O. Collins, A. De Camp,   "

Lieut. John Lanigan, 2d Regt. Inf.,   "

Lieut. W. J. Onahan, Q. M. 2d Regt. Inf.,   "

The Commission will assemble at Parlor No. 1, Grand Pacific Hotel, on Friday evening, the 1st of December, at eight o'clock, to receive suggestions from the General Commanding, and others who are interested in the passage of appropriate laws. The Commission will report the result of their deliberations, on or before the 25th of December next.

: " By command of   ARTHUR C. DUCAT, *Brig. Genl. Comdg.*

GEO. I. WATERMAN,

Lieut. Col. and Asst. Adj'. Genl."

"Official Copy :   HOLDRIDGE O. COLLINS,

Lieut. and A. D. C."

A personal invitation was also sent to Gen. Hilliard requesting his presence and coöperation.

There was, however, no general response to this circular, the attendance being limited entirely to the members of the Staff.   In fact, there seemed to be an unanimous disposition among all subordinate Commanders to avoid any responsibility, and the matter was left entirely with the General, not a single officer replying to his request for advice until the Bill for a law had been drawn, printed and introduced into the Legislature.

The provisions of the Code were agreed upon by Gen. Ducat, Col. Waterman, Gen. Strong, Major Coe and Lieut. Collins of his Staff, after many and anxious deliberations, and Lieut. Collins was requested to draft a Bill for an act revising the Military Code, embodying the suggestions of these gentlemen.

Copies of the Military Codes of all the States noted for their Militia were secured, the different features carefully compared, and liberal extracts were made from such as seemed proper for the status in Illinois.*

---

*The author is under obligations to the Adjutant Generals of Massachusetts, Connecticut, New York, New Jersey, Pennsylvania, Ohio, Michigan and Iowa, for the promptness with which they furnished copies of the Military laws and regulations of their respective States, while he was engaged in drawing this Bill for a new law in Illinois.

Incidental to the preparation of this Bill was the accumulation of a large mass of statistics in relation to the Militia of other States, which was used with great effect before a joint meeting of the Military Committees of the Senate and House, in February, 1877.

The following circular had been prepared and sent to all Military organizations in the State.

" CHICAGO, ILL., Oct. 15, 1876.

To the members of all organized Companies and Battalions of Illinois Militia:

" GENTLEMEN,—In view of the approaching State election, it has been thought advisable to present for your consideration a few suggestions and facts in regard to our State forces.

" It cannot but be known to all of you, that the Militia Law of Illinois is entirely inadequate to secure an effective organization, and that those disciplined troops now existing, which can be relied upon in an emergency, are kept up entirely by private liberality and the personal exertions of individuals.

" The only aid which you have received from the State consists of your arms and equipments. No provisions whatsoever are made in the Statute for rent of Armory, yearly musters, camp equipage and compensation for time when called out by General Orders.

" At the last session of our Legislature, a Bill was introduced in which was embodied a few of the features of the Military Codes of other States, but owing to a want of sufficient attention or the part of its friends, and for other reasons, upon which it is not necessary to dwell, the Bill failed to pass.

" At our next Legislature a new Militia Bill will be introduced, of which the principle features will be a yearly appropriation to meet the expenses for rent of armories, ordnance stores, camp equipage and transportation of all Battalions for

at least one yearly muster, and for ammunition and a Rifle Range
for practice, with an allowance *per diem* for every man who
shall turn out upon order, and with such provisions for the
perfection of discipline as may secure an effective and creditable soldiery.

" The States of Massachusetts, New York, Connecticut and
Pennsylvania, each of which can have a fairly organized army
in the field on twenty-four hours notice, owe the excellence of
their Militia to the large appropriations and the fostering care of
these States.

" I need not dwell upon the necessity of a better Militia
organization in Illinois, for it is plain to you all. In case of
any disturbance or riot, especially in our large cities, the community would be comparatively helpless and at the mercy of
mob violence, but for the individual efforts already put forth,
which cannot much longer be sustained without support.

" This circular is sent to all Commanders of Companies
and Battalions throughout the State, in the earnest hope that
this movement will have the hearty co-operation of all. If
every Company throughout Illinois, *as a body*, will take such
action, so that it may be known that its influence will be given
to that candidate only for the Legislature who will *pledge
himself* to support a new Militia Bill, it will be carried by an
overwhelming majority, and we shall enter upon an entirely
new phase of Military experience.

" The General commanding, hopes to be able to announce
before long that all infantry troops, without exception, will be
armed with the Government breech-loader, and that a general
muster will be had as early as the summer of 1877.

" Relying upon you thoroughly, I have the honor to be,
Very Respectfully,
Your obedient Servant,
ARTHUR C. DUCAT,
Brig. General."

Many encouraging replies were received, and a large proportion of the gentlemen returned as members of the Legislature in the November election, was pledged to vote for a new law.

The Thirtieth General Assembly of Illinois was convened at Springfield on Monday January 8, 1877, and upon final organization the Committees on Military Affairs were as follows:

House—Henry H. Evans, of Kane, Chairman ; E. K. Westfall and Charles H. Whitaker, of McDonough ; George H. Hollister, of Winnebago; Peter Philips, of Franklin; Wm. H. Woodard, of Jackson; Cornelius Rourke, of Menard; Wm. T. McCreery, of Schuyler, and Wm. H. Thompson, George C. Klehm and Arno Voss, of Cook.

Senate—Martin A. DeLaney, of Cook, Chairman ; George W. Herdman, of Jersey; O. V. Smith, of Lawrence; John S. Lee, of Peoria; Bernard Arntzen, of Adams; Luther Dearborn, of Mason; Charles E. McDowell, of White; John T. Morgan of Warren; Henry D. Dement, of Lee; Albert O. Marshall, of Will; Benjamin C. Talliferro, of Mercer, and Miles Kehoe and Daniel N. Bash, of Cook.

The Bill for a new Militia Code having received the approval of many gentlemen of thorough military experience to whom it had been submitted, was carefully transcribed and transmitted to the Adjutant General in the following enclosure:

"CHICAGO, Dec. 21, 1876.

" GENL. H. HILLIARD, *Adjutant General:*

"*Dear General,*—Herewith please find copy of proposed 'Military Code' for the State, just finished. We are poor.

Can't you have this printed as a Bill ready to submit—copies enough for each member of House and Senate and 200 to spare, and very much oblige us? –

"This wants to be done just as soon as possible. Please let me hear from you. I have a note from the Governor that he will meet me to-morrow. I am doing all I can.*

Yours as ever,

ARTHUR C. DUCAT,

Brig. Genl. Comg."

Gen. Hilliard delivered the Bill to Mr. Joseph J. Kearney, of Cook, who presented it to the House on January 16, 1877, when it was referred to the Committee on Militia.

The Adjutant General was dissatisfied with many of the provisions of the proposed law. He desired to have his rank raised to Major General, and to remain Quartermaster General and Inspector General, as under the old law. In his letters of January 26th, 30th and 31st, 1877, he made several suggestions for amendments and changes, and he seemed disposed to make no efforts in its behalf unless his wishes were carried out. In fact, no one seemed to take any further interest in the matter. The Committee failed to report and it appeared as if the Bill would be " buried in the Committee."

The following letter was written by Gen. Ducat :

" CHICAGO, Feb. 1, 1877.

" GEN. H. HILLIARD, *Adjt. Gen. Illinois:*

" *Dear Sir,* — Your communications of Jan. 26, Jan. 30 and Jan. 31, were duly received, and as it appears that we

---

* The author has now in his possession the letter-press copy of the original Bill forwarded in the above letter.

are beginning to get into deep water in regard to our Militia Bill, I wish to make a few suggestions, so that you may understand the position I take in this matter, and that we may not, while desiring the same end, use our exertions so as to defeat the end sought, by a lack of unity.

"Before this bill was drawn, a circular, dated Chicago, Nov. 25, 1876, was issued by me, appointing a Commission, consisting of officers—1st, from my Staff; 2d, from the 1st Regiment; 3d, from the 2d Regiment; 4th, from the 3d Regimen ; 5th, from the 4th Regiment; 6th, from the 5th Regiment; and 7th, from the Company of Cavalry in Chicago—to meet and draw such a Bill, or furnish suggestions for a Bill that would be satisfactory, and, as near as possible, meet the wishes of these organized Regiments. A letter was sent to you, inviting your aid and counsel.

"Although repeatedly invited and urged by me to attend to this matter, I regret to say that, outside of my personal staff, *not one* of the gentlemen appointed paid any attention to the matter.

"There was nothing left for me to do but to get up a Bill myself, or let the matter entirely go by default. The result was that, by giving my personal attention to the matter, and being seconded by the suggestions of my staff, I fixed upon the present bill, now in your hands.

"We none of us think it perfect. On the contrary, we all recognize that it is far from what we need, and what the great State of Illinois should enact ; but the point is to get *something* passed as an entering wedge, which can be amended and improved in the future.

"I very much regret to learn that letters have been sent to members of the Senate and House, finding fault with the Bill and insisting upon amendments; in one particular, by a gentleman who was appointed on that Commission, and who failed to give me any suggestions whatsoever.

"A point is made that a *per diem* of *one dollar*, at least, should be made for each man while in encampment. This subject was thoroughly discussed at the time we settled upon the provisions of the Bill, and this is the conclusion at which we arrived, viz.: Suppose that at the next encampment we have 10,000 men in our active Militia. It will cost *at least* $20,000 to transport to and from encampment, and properly feed such a number for six days. Suppose you pay each man one dollar per day; it would make a total cost for feeding, transportation and pay, of $80,000, of which $60,000 will be for pay. Now, while six dollars will not amount to much to any one man, if we take $60,000 out of our Military fund, we probably will have nothing left to carry on the other necessary portions of the yearly duties. I cite the above case only to show how apt some persons are to rush forward with amendments, without considering the matter.

"I have no doubt many letters suggesting amendments have been written. I wish to say, emphatically, that it is now *too late*. These suggestions should have been made before; and just as sure as members commence loading down our Bill with amendments from different Regiments, just so sure they will sink it so deep that it will never rise to the surface again.

"The greatest pressure should be brought to bear upon the House and Senate to pass it quietly, without stirring up any feeling from the Country delegations, and to get it through as soon as possible.

"When we have it enacted as a law, then come forward with amendments. This we hope and expect will be done. We can get a good Bill only by successive and repeated amendments. Where the Bill is found deficient in its practical operations, there amend; but now, in the present financial condition of the country, any wrangle over the Bill, in either House or Senate, will kill the appropriation.

"I have a further suggestion to make. I wish you would

get the Committees of the Senate and House to fix upon a day
for a joint meeting—any time will suit me, except Feb. 7,
8 and 9—at which time I will come to Springfield with documents and statistics, and see if we cannot make them understand the necessities of this Bill.

" Mr. Collins is now engaged upon a report of what has been
done in New York, Connecticut, Massachusetts, Pennsylvania
and Iowa; and I think the figures which he will show will have
a good effect before the Committees.   I shall bring down with
me other gentlemen ; and if·we can persuade these Committees to recommend our Bill, then we will follow out your suggestions, and assemble at Springfield a large delegation of officers from all parts of the State, and lobby our Bill through.

" I earnestly beg of you to make this appointment for me,
and also not to take any steps without letting me know of your
purpose.   I think your suggestion of a meeting of officers an
excellent one, and it certainly would have a very great effect.
But the *work* must be done before the Committees.

" I have the honor to be,

Yours very respectfully.

ARTHUR C. DUCAT,

Brig. General."

" HOLDRIDGE O. COLLINS, *A. A. G.*"

Mr. De Laney, Chairman of the Senate Committee
on Militia, wrote the following letter:

"SPRINGFIELD, Feb. 22, 1877.

H. O. Collins, Esq.:

" *Dear Sir,*—Who is attending to your Military Bill in the
House?   It should be pushed—if not it will fail for want of
time. There should be some one to take the thing in charge. .
.   .   .   .   . I intend to do all I can for the Militia Bill
when it reaches my Committee.

Yours Resptfy.,

M. A. DE LANEY."

Gen. Ducat immediately wrote the following letter to Gen. Hilliard:

"CHICAGO, Feb. 24, 1877.

"*General:* [Quoting Mr. De Laney's letter.] It seems hard after all our labor that this Bill should fail.

"You are on the ground; will you explain the present situation? What can we do here? We have written a Bill; we have communicated with every officer in the State and used our personal influence with Committees, but there seems to be no one in particular to have charge of this Bill.

Yours respectfully,

ARTHUR C. DUCAT,

Brig. Genl."

GEN. H. HILLIARD, *A. G.*,
    Springfield."

As no assurance of any progress could be obtained, Gen. Ducat determined to take the matter in charge himself and see what could be done by a personal appeal to the Committees, through gentlemen immediately representing him.

In the meanwhile, changes had been made upon his Staff.

In January, Col. Otis resigned, and Lieut. Col. George I. Waterman was promoted to be Colonel and Chief of Staff. Lieut. Holdridge O. Collins was promoted to be Lieutenant Colonel and Assistant Adjutant-General, *vice* Waterman promoted, and Samuel Appleton, late Captain, First Regiment, was appointed First Lieutenant, and Aide-de-Camp, *vice* Collins promoted.

Gen. Hilliard finally arranged a joint meeting of the Committees of the Senate and House, and Colonels

Waterman and Collins proceeded to Springfield, where they were given a patient hearing February 28th.

Their representations were carefully considered, and the Bill was subsequently reported back to the House, with the favorable recommendation of the Committee. On March 28, it was ordered to its second reading, after some lively skirmishing and opposition on the part of its enemies, in which Mr. Watkins, of Pulaski, particularly distinguished himself by a facetious speech in support of his amendment, that each Company be provided with 250 musicians.

The Bill was amended and changed materially in some of its features, but was finally passed on April 12th, owing to the watchfulness and efficiency of Mr. Evans, Mr. Westfall and Mr. Crocker, and it went to the Senate, where Mr. De Laney took the matter in charge, and his Committee reported back the Bill on April 20th, " with the recommendation that it do pass."

Great anxiety about the fate of the Bill had been felt throughout the State, more particularly in Chicago, and the following letter from Gen. Hilliard was received with great satisfaction:

"ADJUTANT GENERAL'S OFFICE,
SPRINGFIELD, April 21st, 1877.

Col. GEO. I. WATERMAN,

86 La Salle St., Chicago:

" *Colonel*,—The " Bill " has passed 1st reading in the Senate, was considered in Committee yesterday and ordered printed for a 2d reading early next week. I am inclined to think that if the Cook County Senators, and especially Mr. De Laney, will pull together and urge it strongly, and bring it up early next week, it will pass. Have them urged to keep off all amendments, but to pass it as it comes from the House. If it goes back there, it may catch a defeat. It is all cut up now so that "Collins" would not know his Bill, but the tax is fixed at 1-20 of a mill, and if it passes we can build upon it hereafter.

Yours Respy,

H. HILLIARD."

The friendly exertions of Senators Lee and Bash, and the rulings of Senator William E. Shutt (whose name is indicative of the summary and effectual manner with which he strangled all dilatory motions), carried the Bill through the dangers of the second reading on May 8, and on May 14, the Bill was finally passed, receiving Governor Cullom's approval, May 18, and it went into effect the following July 1, 1877.

The enactment of the Statute was announced in the following order:

" STATE OF ILLINOIS, ADJUTANT GENERAL'S OFFICE.

SPRINGFIELD, ILL., May 25, 1877.

" The Commander-in-Chief congratulates the members of the Illinois National Guard, on the passage of a State Military Code by the Thirtieth General Assembly, which has received the Executive sanction and is therefore a law. It now becomes your duty to show by your zeal and devotion to duty, your disposition to satisfy the people and their representatives that this favor has not been undeserved.

Relying on your fidelity, the Commander-in-Chief is confident that the expectations of the people of Illinois will not be disappointed, and that the near future will find the State troops of Illinois in a position of proud prominence among the volunteer forces of the Nation.

By order of the Commander-in-Chief.

H. HILLIARD, *Adjutant General.*"

One of the principal features of the new law was the assignment of the entire Militia into Three Brigades, forming one Division, the command of which was given to Gen Ducat, as a matter of course.

He received official notice of his promotion in the following communications:

"GENERAL HEADQUARTERS, STATE OF ILLINOIS.
Adjutant General's Office.
SPRINGFIELD, July 7th, 1877.
MAJOR GEN. A. C. DUCAT,
Comdg. Division, I. N. G.:

"GENERAL,—I have the honor to say that you have this day been appointed by his Excellency, the Governor and Commander-in-Chief, Major General commanding the Division of Illinois National Guards. I sincerely congratulate you, and more I congratulate the National Guard of this State, on the certainty that the policy which has prevailed heretofore in the management of Military affairs in this State, is to be carried out in the future. As the law gives you the selection of your Staff very properly, you are requested to recommend the gentlemen whom you prefer to fill the positions, when I shall be most happy to issue the necessary Commissions. Your own Commission will be forwarded on Monday.

Very Respy. your Obt. Servt.
H. HILLIARD, ·
Adjt. Gen."

"STATE OF ILLINOIS,
EXECUTIVE DEPARTMENT,
SPRINGFIELD, July 9, 1877.
GENL. ARTHUR C. DUCAT,
Chicago. Ills. :

"DEAR SIR,—I have the honor and pleasure of handing you herewith your Commission as Major General Commanding Division Illinois National Guard.

"Trusting in your fidelity to the interest of the State Militia, and your devotion to the State and Nation, I am,

With Great respect,

Truly yours,

S. M. CULLOM."

IV.

The Division and the Railroad Riots of July, 1877.

HE New Military Code, in Section 1 of Article IV, provided that the Staff of the Commander-in-Chief should consist of an Adjutant General, ranking as a Major General, who should also be *ex-officio* Chief of Staff, Commissary General and Quartermaster General, and such other officers as he might think proper to appoint.

With a liberal interpretation of this provision, Gov. Cullom selected a generous staff, which would have been a credit to the Commander-in-Chief of the combined forces of all the Russias. The following gentlemen were commissioned:

Maj. Gen. Hiram Hilliard, Adjt. Gen., Springfield.
Brig. Gen. Wm. E. Strong, Inspector Gen., Chicago.
    "   Saml. B. Sherer, Chief of Cavalry, Chicago.
    "   Elisha B. Hamilton, Chief of Ordnance, Chicago.
    "   Benson Wood, Judge Advocate Gen., Effingham.
    "   Rufus S. Lord, Surgeon Gen., Springfield.
    "   Louis Schaffner, Paymaster Gen., Chicago.
Colonel Huntington W. Jackson, Aide-de-Camp, Chicago.

" Wm. H. Thompson,	"	"
" Ernst F. C. Klokke	"	"
" Henry H. Evans,	"	Aurora.
" Benjamin F. Sheets,	"	Oregon.
" David O. Reid,	"	Moline.
" Sylvester W. Munn,	"	Joliet.
" Edward P. Durell,	"	Vermont.
" Wm. A. Larimer,	"	Aledo.
" Wm. H. Edgar,	"	Jerseyville.
" Noble B. Wiggins,	"	Springfield.
" Wm. J. Pollock,	"	Ottawa.
" George Scroggs,	"	Champaign.
" John J. Brenhalt,	"	Alton.
" Thomas J. Golden,	"	Marshall.
" Geo. W. Johns,	"	Fairfield.
" Willis E. Finch,	"	E. St. Louis
Lieut. Col. Geo. R. Cannon,	"	Chicago.
Major H. Sherman Vail.	"	"
" Wm. T. Vandeveer,	"	Taylorville.
Captain James M. Rice,	"	Peoria.
" A. M. Trimble,	"	Ottawa.
" Geo. W. Akins,	"	Nashville.
" Reed Jones,	"	Joliet.
" Harry F. White,	"	Nokomis.
" Edward F. Gale,	"	Chicago.
First Lieut. Jerry J. Crowley,	"	"
Second Lieut. Wm. T. Hall,	"	"

The Adjutant General and Inspector General were the only officers of the above Staff to whom particular allusion was made in the Statute, these positions being *sui generis*, and requiring special provisions.

Under the old law, the Adjutant General was also the Inspector General, but now the Inspector General's department was created upon an independent basis, and turned over to the exclusive control of Brig. Gen. Strong. The Major General was given an Assistant Inspector, with rank of Lieutenant Colonel, but as Gen. Strong, by General Order No. 2, under date July 11, 1877, was assigned for duty on the Division Staff, Gen. Ducat regarded the office of Assistant Inspector as superfluous, and he never filled the vacancy.

Gov. Cullom commissioned the following gentlemen as the general officers commanding the Militia:

MAJOR GENERAL.
ARTHUR C DUCAT, Chicago.

BRIGADIER GENERALS.
Joseph T. Torrence, First Brigade, Chicago.
Erastus N. Bates, Second Brigade, Springfield.
Charles W. Pavey, Third Brigade, Mount Vernon.

The first Staff of the Division was composed of:

Colonel Geo. I. Waterman, Chief of Staff.
Brig. Gen. Wm. E. Strong, by assignment, Inspector Gen.
Lieut. Col. Holdridge O. Collins, Asst. Adjt. Gen.
"   "   Jerome F. Weeks, Surgeon.
Major Albert L. Coe, Quartermaster.
"   Henry B. Maxwell, Commissary.
"   Henry B. Whitehouse, Paymaster.
Captain Samuel Appleton, Aide-de-Çamp.
"   David H. Gile,   "

The position of Judge Advocate was left temporarily vacant. Subsequently changes were made, and at the time of the resignation of Gen. Ducat, in June, 1879, his Staff was composed as follows:

Colonel Percy P. Oldershaw, Chief of Staff.
Brig. Gen. Wm. E. Strong, Inspector General.
Lieut. Col. Samuel Appleton, Asst. Adjt. Gen.
"   "   Jerome F. Weeks, Surgeon.
Major Albert L. Coe, Quartermaster.
    "   Henry B. Maxwell, Commissary.
    "   Henry B. Whitehouse, Paymaster.
    "   Holdridge O. Collins, Judge Advocate.

The positions of Aides-de-Camp being also vacant.

In the original draft of the new Military Code, the rank of all the Staff officers of the Division and Brigades was generally modelled after the New York Code, and was in almost every case higher than the corresponding office in the Regular Army. The Legislature became wearied of cutting down, trimming and amending the Bill when progress had been made through about half of its provisions, and the remainder was passed without change and without consideration as to any inconsistencies that might exist. The rank of the Division Judge Advocate in the Bill as introduced, was Colonel. This was reduced to Major, and the result was, that the rank of the Brigade Judge Advocate was left higher by one grade than the Division Judge Advocate, and the anomaly was created of a Major passing upon the acts of Lieutenant Colonels.

The following officers composed the Staffs of the several Brigades:

FIRST BRIGADE.

Lieut. Col. Henry A. Huntington, Asst. Adjt. Gen., who was succeeded by Geo. R. Cannon

Lieut. Col. Elijah B. Sherman, Judge Advocate.

Major John Lanigan, Inspector.

Major Fernand Henrotin, Surgeon.

Captain Joseph Kirkland, Quartermaster, who was succeeded by William C. Lyon.

Captain Charles H. Taylor, Commissary.

First Lieut. W. S. Scribner, Aide-de-Camp.

First Lieut. Edward T. Sawyer, Aide-de-Camp.
    All of Chicago.

SECOND BRIGADE.

Lieut. Col. Jas. F. McNeill, Asst. Adjt. Gen., Springfield, succeeded by Jasper N. Reece.

Lieut. Col. Orin P. Cooley, Judge Advocate, Oneida.

Major Gustavus S. Dana, Inspector, Springfield.

Major Thomas G. Black, Surgeon, Clayton.

Captain Charles F. Mills, Quartermaster, Springfield.

Captain Wm. F. Smith, Commissary,   ''

First Lieut. William L. Distin, Aide-de-Camp, Quincy.

In November, 1877, Gen. Bates resigned, and Jasper N. Reece was commissioned Brigadier General of the Second Brigade. He made but few changes upon his Staff, retaining the same gentlemen, and making the following new appointments:

Lieut. Col. Chas. F. Mills, Asst. Adjt. Gen., Springfield.

Captain George C. Cole, Quartermaster, Springfield.

First Lieut. Christopher Wolf, Aide-de-Camp, Springfield.

Third Brigade.

Lieut. Col. Albion F. Taylor, Asst. Adj. Gen. Mt. Vernon.
Lieut. Col. Columbus A. Keller, Judge Advocate.
Major Robert B. Stinson, Inspector, Anna.
Major Augustus De Foe, Surgeon, McLeansboro.
Captain Wm. Swanwick, Quartermaster, Chester.
Captain Daniel Berry, Commissary, Carmi.
First Lieut. John B. Crowder, Aide-de-Camp, Mt. Vernon.
First Lieut. Wm. Hendrickson, Aide-de-Camp, Marion.

The Biennial Report of the Adjutant General, in January, 1877, showed that when Gen. Ducat was appointed Brigadier General, the State Militia consisted of 895 men only. The First Regiment, at Chicago, was the only Battalion organization, being composed of eight Companies, the rest of the force being members of independent, detached and unassigned Companies.

In September, 1876, Gen. Ducat had organized a Brigade, composed of 5,145 men and officers, assigned to Seven Regiments, three Battalions and eight detached Companies, among which were one Company of Cavalry, at Chicago, and one Battery of two pieces, at Danville. After the enactment of the new Code, which imposed a tax for the payment of the most necessary expenses, the existing Regiments were rapidly recruited to a maximum, and the organization of other Regiments and Battalions was commenced.

General Order No. 3 was issued from the Adjutant General's Office, under date July 11, 1877, assigning the forces to Brigades as follows:

First Brigade.

First, Second, Third, Ninth and Tenth Regiments Infantry, Company A, Light Cavalry, Chicago, and Battery A, Danville

SECOND BRIGADE.

Fourth, Fifth, Sixth, Seventh and Eighth Regiments Infantry.

THIRD BRIGADE.   •

All Companies then organized and in process of organization south of the Ohio and Mississippi Railroad.

These preliminary steps for carrying out the provisions of the Code had scarcely been taken, when the news of the terrible reign of lawlessness at Pittsburg and Baltimore, on July 21st and 22d, was flashed through the State, and the attention of the entire Country became directed to Chicago, as the great center of the vast Railroad system of the Northwest. There was a very general feeling that the Railroads had acted with oppression towards their employes, and the public almost universally sympathized with these laborers and mechanics.

It was evident that unless the troubles were checked at this point, the Country would be thrown into a revolution. The time had come for the Militia to show whether it were capable of the stern duty and exacting dicripline of the soldier.

Sunday and Monday, July 22d and 23d, were days of feverish uncertainty and repressed excitement at Chicago, Peoria, Galesburg and East St. Louis. The forces throughout the State were ordered under arms. By prompt action, the National Blues, Emmet Guards and Veteran Guards, under the command of their respective officers, quelled an outbreak at Peoria in short order, and the Emmet Guards proceeded to Galesburg, where an incipient riot, directed against the Railroad works, was summarily surpressed.

Gen. Bates took personal command of the National
Blues and Veteran Guards of Peoria, the Taylorville
Guards, Morgan Cadets of Jacksonville, and the Veteran
and National Guards of Quincy, and proceeded to East
St. Louis, where he was joined, July 28th, by Gen.
Pavey, in command of the Belleville Guards and Mt.Ver-
non Guards. Governor Cullom was present at this
place and under his personal direction, by the exercise
of mild firmness, order was restored in a very dangerous
community, without the loss of life or property.

Other points of railroad interests — La Salle, Mat-
toon, Pana, Decatur, Bloomington, Streator and Altona
— were fully protected by the local Militia Commands,
and Chicago was the only place in the State where the
situation at any time became alarming.

On Monday, July 23d, the entire forces in Chicago,
consisting of the First and Second Regiments of Infantry
and one Company of Cavalry, were ordered to hold
themselves ready for instant service. The Bohemian
Guards were disarmed and ultimately disbanded, some
of their officers being found active leaders of the mob.

The following despatch was received:

" SPRINGFIELD, ILL., July 23, 1877.
GEN. A. C. DUCAT:

"Under the charter of cities and towns, the Mayor, subject
to the Governor, has the power to call out the Militia. Please
confer with him.

S. M. Cullom, *Governor.*"

Gen. Ducat called upon Mayor Monroe Heath and
tendered to him the aid of the entire local command.
Mr. Heath, however, declined to avail himself of this

assistance, stating that he did not wish the troops to be seen on the streets, as he believed the disastrous results of the riots at Pittsburgh, were owing principally to the unwarranted interference of the Militia, and he felt confident of being able to suppress all disturbances in Chicago with the Police force. The same evening, a meeting of workingmen was held at the corner of Madison and Market streets, at which the Communistic element predominated, but no overt act of violence was committed. On Tuesday morning, however, mobs began to assemble in the West Division on Halsted, Canal and Kinzie streets, compelling workingmen in the lumber and manufacturing districts to quit work. These laborers helped to swell the mobs, and nearly the entire Police force of the City was ordered to this district.

The following message was sent in the morning:

"CHICAGO, July 24th, 1877.

MAJ. GEN. H. HILLIARD,
    Adjutant General, Springfield:

" I don't think the authorities here fully appreciate the gravity of the situation. Although the City was quiet last night and this morning, I believe trouble will occur here about to-morrow. I recommend the immediate concentration of State troops here that can be spared from other points, including the Danville Battery. The Railroads may fail us, and it will be much easier to send troops out, than to get them in. Think of this. I believe, with the example of other cities before us, this action is nothing more than our clear duty. Answer.

DUCAT, *Major General Commanding.*

Mayor Heath, upon being informed by Gen. Ducat of the proposed movement, stated emphatically that he did not think it necessary, and he requested that no more troops be brought to the city. Whereupon the following message was sent:

"CHICAGO, July 24, 1877.

To MAJ. GEN. HILLIARD, *Springfield:*

"Have consulted with the Mayor. He is opposed to bringing in troops. Hold them ready, nevertheless.

DUCAT, *Maj. Gen. Commanding.*"

The entire police force had been on active duty over a day, fighting the mobs in the West Division. All the Station houses were filled with rioters who had been arrested, and now reports came that the police were exhausted and were being overpowered by numbers.

Up to Wednesday the 25th, the Mayor had declined to make a formal call for the use of the troops, but, urged by the unwise counsel of a few panic-stricken citizens, who were large property owners, he made frequent verbal requests that the forces should be distributed around the city and suburbs for the protection of individual interests.

Gen. Ducat, refused to divide his forces into small detachments, or to permit any interference with his command. He notified the Mayor that he had been prepared to disperse all mobs, since the outbreak, and he would move the instant he obtained a request or permission to march upon the streets; but he was the judge as to the manner in which the Military should act, and he should exercise his own discretion in that respect.

Late in the evening of the 25th, it became evident at Division Headquarters that the Civil Authorities were powerless to restore order, and that the Mayor would be compelled to call for help.

Gen. Ducat moved the Second Regiment from its Armory on West Jackson street to the Rock Island Railroad Depot, and the First Regiment was marched to the Exposition Building, both these places being more available for concerted action and much more desirable for the health of the troops, suffering as they were from heat in their armories. The troops bivouacked in these buildings for the night, and were ready for the speedy demand which was made for their services.

Early Thursday morning the following was received:

"MAYOR'S OFFICE,
CHICAGO, July 26, 1877.
MAJOR GENERAL ARTHUR C. DUCAT:
"You are hereby authorized to use whatever Military you have in this city subject to your command, to suppress the riots now in progress in different parts of the city, subject to my orders.
M. HEATH, *Mayor.*"

Immediately, the Second Regiment, commanded by Lieut. Col. James Quirk, and the First Regiment, under the command of Lieut. Col. S. B. Sherer (Col. McClurg being at this time in Europe), were marched to the heart of the riotous district in the West Division, and during the day they scattered and dispersed all the mobs and riotous assemblages. They were several times attacked, and under less cool Commanders, the day might have had a bloody ending, as both commands were several times placed in situations where a volley would have been justified. Cols. Quirk and Sherer, however, sternly repressed all firing, the bayonet only being used, and the sun went down without the loss of a life caused by the Militia.

Late in the afternoon, the Second Regiment was stationed at the Halsted Street viaduct, and the First within supporting distance, on Twelfth Street, near the river. The two Regiments remained on duty at these posts all night. Three old cannon belonging to the State, had been found in the possession of the City, and Col. Bolton hastily organized a volunteer Municipal Battery, which did excellent service. One gun was stationed with the First Regiment, so as to command the Twelfth Street bridge, and a second gun was annexed to Col. Quirk's command, at the Sixteenth Street viaduct. The First Regiment was not molested after dark, but an attack was made upon the Second during the night by a mob, which, however, was dispersed by two volleys, the first fired at 9:10 P.M., and the second at 10:30 P. M.

On Thursday, the 26th, six companies of the Ninth Infantry and two companies of the Twenty-second Infantry U. S. Army, arrived in Chicago. They were stationed at several points throughout the City, and at the Stock Yards, and their presence did much to restore confidence.

In the afternoon of Friday, the 27th, all disturbances in the City having ceased, the two Regiments were marched back to their temporary armories, and Chicago resumed her wonted peaceful aspect.

On July 24th, Gov. Cullom telegraphed that there was trouble brewing among the miners at Braidwood, a small coal mining Station on the Chicago and Alton Railroad.

The proprietors of the mine had lately imported several hundred negroes from the South as laborers, much to the dissatisfaction of a large foreign element which had been theretofore employed in the mines, and they seized upon the present opportunity to rise against the colored people, and by July 28th, they had driven them, with their women and children, from their homes, refusing to allow them to return even to obtain food and clothing.

About 5 o'clock P. M., on July 27th, peremptory orders came from Gov. Cullom, to send a strong force for their protection, and Gen. Ducat immediately made his arrangements to go in person, leaving Gen. Torrence with the Second Regiment, in command of the City. At 10 o'clock P. M., telegrams were sent to Col. J. W. R. Stambaugh, at Sterling, and the Commanding officers of Companies of his Regiment, to report immediately at Chicago, and at five o'clock next morning, the Rockford, Creston, La Salle, Sycamore (2), and Aurora Companies, with Col. Stambaugh at their head, presented themselves at Division Headquarters in Chicago, fully armed and equipped for service. Regular troops with transportation facilities could not have acted with greater despatch, and Col. Stambaugh and his Third Regiment have the credit of performing the neatest act of soldiership during the troubles.

The First and Third Regiments were embarked on the train, and leaving Chicago at 1 P. M., on Saturday, the command arrived at Braidwood at 5 P. M., having taken up at Joliet two companies of the Tenth Battalion, under Lieut. Col. Parsons, and the Joliet Battery under Capt. J. Q. A. King.

Short work was made with the riotous elements at Braidwood. They were quickly disarmed and dispersed; the colored people were restored to their homes and usual avocations, and furnished with rations for one day from the Military supplies, as they were entirely destitute.

Order was fully established by Sunday evening, and on Monday, July 30, leaving a small detachment of the Tenth Battalion to preserve order at Braidwood, the command returned to Chicago, and was dismissed from further duty, all disturbances having ceased throughout the State.

The following General Orders were published:

"GENERAL HEADQUARTERS, STATE OF ILLINOIS,
ADJUTANT GENERAL'S OFFICE.
SPRINGFIELD, August 4, 1877.

General Orders No. 7.

" The Commander-in-Chief congratulates the Illinois National Guard on the restoration of law and order throughout the length and breadth of the State.

" To the Military of the Commonwealth is due the thanks of the people for the alacrity with which they obeyed the summons to duty; and the zeal which characterized their movements has been the subject of favorable comment from press and people. As an important factor in the preservation of the peace, you have fully justified the hope entertained by your friends, and established a just right to future recognition by the law making power of the State.

" The Commander-in-Chief trusts that the necessity may never again arise for a similar use of the power of the State, but should it, he relies confidently on your courage and patriotism.

" By order of the Governor and Commander-in-Chief.

H. HILLIARD,
Adjutant General."

" DIVISION HEADQUARTERS, ILLINOIS NATIONAL GUARD.

CHICAGO, August 6, 1877.

General Orders No. 4.

" I.   Generals Commanding Brigades of the Illinois National Guard will issue and publish an order dismissing their troops to their respective homes.

" II.   General Torrence Commanding the First Brigade will hold the detachment of his command now at Braidwood, at that point until further orders.

" III.   The General Commanding the Division takes great pleasure and pride in thanking the troops in the name of the Governor and the law and order loving people of the State, and in his own behalf, for their prompt and patriotic response to the first call of duty which has been made upon them for active Military service   The cheerful and courageous obedience to all the orders given, and the great patience manifested under the most trying circumstances, have made them worthy the pride of every good citizen of the State.

" The troops of the First Brigade came more immediately under the observation of the General Commanding, and he compliments Gen. Torrence, upon the steady, unwavering and untiring conduct of the First and Second Regiments, and for the alacrity with which the Third Regiment and Tenth Battalion concentrated and reported their commands.   They will be appreciated.

ARTHUR C. DUCAT,

Major General Commanding.

GEORGE I. WATERMAN,

Colonel and Chief of Staff.

Official .

HOLDRIDGE O. COLLINS,

Lieut. Col. and Asst. Adjt. Gen."

The public attention had been particularly attracted toward the Militia by reason of its good service during the riots, and large numbers of recruits were enlisted all over the State.

The work of perfecting the organization of the new Brigades into a Division, which had been interrupted so soon after the law went into effect, was now resumed, and carried out with vigor. In Chicago, three new companies of Cavalry were raised, forming a Battalion of four Companies, commanded by Major Dominick Welter, and all fully armed and equipped, with an ample provision, by private subscription, for being mounted when called upon for service, and two Battalions of Infantry were recruited,—the Sixth, with six Companies, commanded by Lieut. Col. Moses W. Powell; and the Sixteenth, colored, of four Companies, under the command of Major Theodore C. Hubbard.

They were provided with uniforms and armories by private subscription, the State furnishing the arms and equipments.

During the Summers of 1877 and 1878, many other Regiments and Battalions of Infantry were successfully recruited and enrolled throughout the State. Two additional Batteries of Artillery were perfected—B, at Springfield, under Capt. John G. Mack, and C, at Joliet, commanded by Capt. Mansfield Young; and Gen. Ducat made great exertions to obtain a Battery at Chicago. Gen. Sheridan very kindly interested himself in the matter, and through him negotiations were commenced with the General Government at Washington, for a complete Battery, consisting of two three-inch rifled guns, ordnance pattern; four twelve-pounder, smooth-bore Napoleon guns, and one Gatling gun, calibre forty-five. It was found, however, that no help could be had in this quarter, as Illinois had already overdrawn her quota of arms, and the authorities refused to make any further advancement.

Again the generosity and public spirit of individuals stepped forward and furnished the necessary funds. L. Z. Leiter, Esq., of Chicago, took the lead, and through his means, and the influence of the Citizens' Association, a very complete and satisfactory Battery was purchased, consisting of four twelve-pounder Napoleon guns, and one Gatling gun, with equipments, of which Maj. Edgar P. Tobey was given the command.

Gen. Ducat induced all the Commands to unite in an effort to secure a large General Armory, with drill-sheds of sufficient size to permit the evolutions of a Regiment; but, although plans were made and many meetings held, the money could not be raised, and the attempt was abandoned.

In the month of September, 1877, the first general inspection of the troops, under the new law, was made according to the directions of Gen. Strong. His report of this inspection, and of the inspection held September, 1878, is to be found in the Biennial Report of the Adjutant General for 1877 and 1878. (*Vide* pp. 57–78.)

In October, 1877, arose the first occasion to make use of the provisions as to Courts Martial.

Special order No. 10, from Division Headquarters, under date October 8th, was issued, commanding a Court Martial at Altona, Knox County, for the trial of the First Lieutenant of Company C, Fourth Regiment, upon charges and specifications duly presented. The Court assembled October 23d, with Maj. William Jackson, Fourth Regiment, as President; and after a careful consideration of the case, the Lieutenant was sentenced to be cashiered, which sentence was approved by Gov. Cullom, in General Court Martial Order, No. 1, dated Springfield, December 17, 1877.

In the perfecting of the Division, Gen. Ducat was most materially assisted by Colonels C. M. Brazee, Third Regiment; William Whitney, Fourth Regiment; William Hanna, Eighth Regiment; M. H. Peters, Ninth Regiment; J. B. Parsons, Tenth Regiment; and John B. Fithian, Twelfth Regiment. These officers brought their several commands to a high condition of discipline, which gave them rank among the first in the State.

Col. Brazee, of Rockford, by his untiring labors, has preserved a very great cordiality of feeling between men and officers, and his Regiment is invariably unanimous on all questions of their general interest. It ranks first in numbers and second in drill in the State.

Colonels Parsons and Fithian carried their commands successfully through the troubles of 1877–1878, caused by the lack of money for expenses, and the repeated changes in the Companies forming their Regiments. In reörganizing the Division, one of the principal objects aimed at, was the assignment of neighboring Companies to the same Regiment, and, as a consequence, the complexion of many commands was almost entirely changed. But this eventually resulted in great benefit, and brought about a more united feeling in the respective Regiments and Battalions.

The weak points of the new Code soon became apparent.

It contained some inconsistences and the annual tax of one-twentieth of a mill was entirely too small to satisfy the demands of the service. It was the intention to follow the example of New York, and obtain a better law by gradual amendments for larger appropriations. The tax of one mill asked in the Bill, as introduced, had been reduced, as it was difficult to induce " the Country members" of the Legislature to vote any money for Militia purposes.

In the latter part of 1877, it was thought best to call a general meeting of officers to discuss the matter, and a circular, dated December 8, 1877, was issued from Springfield by a committee of officers, headed by Adjt. Gen. Hilliard, and Brig. Gen. Reece of the Second Brigade, suggesting that a Convention be called at Springfield the following month.

The idea met with universal approval, and on January 15, 1878, probably the largest assembly of Militia officers ever held in Illinois, was called to order by Gen. Hilliard in the Chamber of the House of Representatives.

Governor Cullom welcomed them in a very graceful speech of congratulations upon their successful work, and thanks for their services during the riots.

Gen. Ducat was elected President, with Brig. Gens. Torrence, Pavey and Reece as Vice-Presidents.

All matters pertaining to the general welfare and advancement of the service were freely discussed, and it was decided that a committee should be selected to draw a new Bill for a Militia law, embracing the points determined upon by the Convention.

The President appointed Gen. Hilliard chairman of this Committee, with power to nominate the other members, and the remainder of the Committee as appointed, consisted of Brig. Gen. William E. Strong, of Chicago, Inspector General; Brig. Gen. E. B. Hamilton, of Quincy, Chief of Ordnance; Brig. Gen. Benson Wood, of Effingham, Judge Advocate General; Major R. F. Stinson, of Anna, Inspector of Second Brigade; Lieut. Col. Jerome F. Weeks, Division Surgeon, and Lieut. Col. E. B. Sherman, Judge Advocate First Brigade, both of Chicago.

In the Spring of 1878, Chicago was troubled by a threatened outbreak of the Communistic element. Information was sent to Gen. Ducat, that a plan had been formed to seize the arms of the First and Second Regiments, and burn the Exposition Building and the Railroad property on the Lake Shore. Governor Cullom became satisfied that these fears were not groundless, and by his direction, a guard was kept up during the months of April and May. The Second Regiment abandoned its Armory on West Jackson Street, and for several months had its home at the North End of the Exposition Building. Later it secured another Armory on Randolph Street.

During the Summer of 1878, the Third Regiment was encamped at Sycamore, the Tenth Battalion at Pontiac, and the Twelfth Battalion at Morris, and generally, inspecting, reviewing, drilling and instruction in rifle practice were the order of the day all over the State.

The Biennial Report of the Adjutant General, in January 1879, showed that during 1877 and 1878, the Division had been organized into Three Brigades composed of Eight Regiments of Infantry, Eight Battalions

of Infantry, One Battalion of Cavalry and Three Batteries
o Artillery, with 497 Field, Staff and Line Officers and
6,361 enlisted men, making a total force of 6,858, including
the Commander-in-Chief and Staff.

The Brigade assignments were as follow:

FIRST BRIGADE.

Brig. Gen., Joseph T. Torrence, Chicago.

FIRST REGIMENT.

Colonel, Edgar D. Swain, Chicago.
Lieutenant Colonel, Rudolph Williams, Chicago.
Major, Edwin B. Knox, Chicago.
Companies A, B, C, D, E, F, G, H, I, K.
Forty officers and 488 enlisted men.

SECOND REGIMENT.

Colonel, James Quirk, Chicago.
Lieut. Colonel, Wm. P. Rend, Chicago.
Major, Peter J. Hennessey, Chicago.
Companies A, B, C, D, E, F, G.
Twenty-three officers and 358 enlisted men.

THIRD REGIMENT.

Colonel, C. M. Brazee, Rockford.
Lieut: Colonel, T. B. Coulter, Aurora.
Major, Oscar W. Phelps, Sycamore.
Companies A, B, C, D, E, F, G, H, I, K.
Thirty-three officers and 527 enlisted men.

SIXTH BATTALION.

Lieut. Col., Moses W. Powell, Chicago.
Major, Benjamin R. DeYoung, Chicago.
Companies A, B, C, D, E, F.
Nineteen officers and 233 enlisted men.

NINTH BATTALION.

Lieut. Col., M. H. Peters, Watseka.
Major, Amos S. Cowan, Danville.
Companies A, B, C, D, E, F.
Twenty-one officers and 256 enlisted men.

TENTH BATTALION.

Lieut. Col., J. B. Parsons, Dwight.
Major, John K. Howard, Odell.
Companies A, B, C, D, E, F.
Twenty-one officers and 309 enlisted men.

TWELFTH BATTALION.

Lieut. Col., John B. Fithian, Joliet.
Major, Wm. G. Coulter, La Salle.
Companies A, B, C, D, E, F.
Twenty-one officers and 259 enlisted men.

SIXTEENTH (COLORED) BATTALION.

Major, Theodore C. Hubbard, Chicago.
Companies A and B, of Chicago, Clark County
Guards, of Marshall, and Cumberland County Guards,
of Greenup.
Eleven officers and 106 enlisted men.

First Battalion Cavalry.

Major, Dominick Welter, Chicago.
Companies A, B, C, D.
Twelve officers and 209 enlisted men.

ARTILLERY.

*Battery A.

Captain, Edwin Winter, Danville.
Three officers and 48 enlisted men.

Battery C.

Captain, Mansfield Young, Joliet.
Three officers and 61 enlisted men.
Making the total strength of the Brigade, 203 officers
and 2,854 enlisted men.

SECOND BRIGADE.

Brig. Gen., Jasper N. Reece, Springfield.

Fourth Regiment.

Colonel, Wm. Whiting, Altona.
Lieut. Colonel, Wm. Jackson, Toulon.
Major, O. L. Higgins, Oneida.
Companies A, B, C, D, E, F, G, II, I.
Twenty-eight officers and 378 enlisted men.

Fifth Regiment.

Colonel, James II. Barkley, Springfield.
Lieut. Colonel, Cornelius Rourke, Petersburg.

Major, Jas. F. McNeil, Springfield.
Companies A, B, C, D, E, F, G, H, I, K.
Forty officers and 629 enlisted men.

ATTACHED.

Decatur Grenadiers, Capt., C. M. Durfee.
Virginia Lippincott Guards, Capt., Wm. Murray.
Three officers and 59 enlisted men.

SEVENTH REGIMENT.

Colonel, Isaac Taylor, Peoria.
Lieut. Colonel, John S. Kirk, Havana.
Major, K. S. Conklin, Pekin.
Companies A, B, C, D, E, F, G, H, I, K.
Thirty-seven officers and 539 enlisted men.

EIGHTH REGIMENT.

Colonel, Wm. Hanna, Keokuk Junction.
Lieut. Colonel, C. S. Hickman, Quincy.
Major, C. Y. Long, Carthage.
Companies A, B, C, D, E, F, G, H, I, K.
Forty officers and 627 enlisted men.

ATTACHED.

Pittsfield Guards, Capt., Wm. N. Shibley.

FOURTEENTH BATTALION.

Lieut. Col., Wm. P. Butler, Rock Island.
Major, J. B. Magill, Moline.
Companies A, B, C, D, E.
Fifteen officers and 178 enlisted men.

Fifteenth Battalion.

Lieut. Col., James T. Cooper, Alton.
Major, Walter E. Carlin, Jerseyville.
Companies A, B, C, D, E, F.
Twenty-two officers and 374 enlisted men.

ARTILLERY.

Battery B.

Captain, John G. Mack, Springfield.
Total force of Brigade, 185 officers and 2,784 enlisted men.

THIRD BRIGADE.

Brig. Gen., Charles W. Pavey, Mt. Vernon.

Eleventh Regiment.

Col., Cassimer Andel, Belleville.
Lieut. Col., Louis Krughoff, Nashville.
Major, James Hitchcock, Mt. Vernon.
Companies A, B, C, D, E, F, G, H, I, K.
Twenty-seven officers and 464 enlisted men.

Thirteenth Battalion.

Lieut. Col., Archibald Spring, Olney.
Major, C. C. Wickersham, Fairfield.
Companies A, B, C, D, E.
Fifteen officers and 259 enlisted men.
Total strength, 42 officers and 723 enlisted men.

Gen. Hilliard pays the following tribute to Generals Strong and Ducat:

"To Brig. Gen. Wm. E. Strong, Inspector General, I feel myself highly indebted, and while the effect of his labors, which are more fully described in his appended report, may not at present be apparent, in the fullness of time, the National Guard of this State will exhibit, by their proficiency, the greatness of the work which he has performed."

.   .   .   .   .

"I take pleasure in acknowledging the eminent services rendered by Maj. Gen. A. C. Ducat, Commanding the Division, as also the services of his various Staff officers. With him and them my intercourse has been pleasant. Their assistance and advice has been constantly at my disposal, and it is due to them for me to say that they have rendered your Excellency, most cheerfully, their hearty aid and concurrence in the work of organization, and in aiding in the preservation of public tranquility." (*Vide*, p. 12.)

In his Biennial message to the Thirty-first General Assembly, Governor Cullom spoke of the Militia in these terms :

"After the era of prosperity which followed the war, there naturally came a period of depression. Hard times set in, and many laboring men connected with Railroads, and manufacturing and mining establishments were thrown out of work, and the wages of those employed were, from time to time, reduced. As a result of this condition of things, they became restless and dissatisfied; disagreements occurred, and frequent strikes followed. Finally in July, 1877, the quiet of the people was suddenly broken, and the business of almost the whole country was stopped by assemblages of men, who, in violation and defiance of law and of the civil authorities, took possession of

Railroads, manufacturing establishments and mines, and forced the owners, and those willing and eager to work, to stop work and submit to the dictation of the rioters.

"So unlooked for were these occurrences, that few of the States had any preparation for them. At some places there was great loss of life and property; but in our own State, with the exception of the sad occurrences of one day in the Streets of Chicago, the whole record of suffering and loss is told when the statement is made that for a week, many of the Railroads, mines and manufacturing establishments were under the rule of lawless men, and the commerce of the State was at a stand still.

"The act passed by the last General Assembly, in 1877, providing for the organization of the Militia, had been in force but a few days, and nothing had been done under it to organize the Military force of the State. There was no adequate preparation for the troubles which so suddenly came upon us. Every military company in the State, however, whether mustered into service or not, and whether armed and equipped or not— none of them being fully equipped for active duty—responded to the call upon them, and held themselves in readiness to go wherever ordered, and to perform any duty, as soldiers, which the exigencies of the time demanded.

"Ammunition was procured with all possible dispatch, and as soon as the National Guard could reach the different points in the State where the rioters were interfering with labor, and in possession of Railroad trains, and manufacturing and mining establishments, all unlawful assemblages were dispersed and business resumed. While the strike and riotous lawlessness resulted in no destruction of property in this State, it cost the State a considerable sum of money, besides the loss sustained by citizens, in the interference with their business.

"The officers and men of the Illinois National Guard are entitled to the heartiest thanks of the people of the State for their prompt and efficient service. As already stated, every

Military organization in the State was called to duty, and was either in active service, or at its Armory waiting orders, for about fifteen days.

"The Railway trains and machine shops and factories, in Chicago, Peoria, Galesburg, Decatur and East St. Louis, were in the hands of the mob, as well as the mines at Braidwood, LaSalle, and some other places; and all these places were urgently demanding a Military force to aid the civil authorities in their efforts to preserve the peace and enforce the law.

"A Military force was placed on duty at all the places named above, with strict orders to act subordinate to and in assistance of the civil authorities.

"Their behaviour throughout was unexceptionable. . . . The occurrences of July, 1877, gave a great impetus to the organization of the Militia, under the existing law. . . . . .

"The suggestions and recommendations of the Adjutant General, in relation to the equipment of the National Guard, so that they may at all times be ready for active duty, the building of a new State Arsenal and the sale of the present one, I most cordially endorse. . . . . . The experience of the last two years confirms my views expressed to the Thirtieth General Assembly."

V.

. ———

The Militia Law of 1879.

———

S Has been intimated, measures were adopted in the winter of 1878, looking toward the securing of amendments to the Code at the next Session of the Legislature.

The Thirty-first General Assembly was convened at Springfield, on Wednesday, January 8, 1879, and the several Military Committees of the House and Senate were appointed, as follows:

Senate–Sylvester W. Munn, of Joliet, Chairman; Benjamin C. Taliaferro, of Keithsburg; Joseph H. Mayborne, of Geneva; Henry D. Dement, of Dixon; Daniel N. Bash, and Sylvester Artley, of Chicago; John R. Marshall, of Yorkville; Milton M. Ford, of Galva; George W. Herdman, of Jerseyville; William H. Neece, of Macomb; Thomas E. Merritt, of Salem; Samuel L. Cheaney, of Harrisburg, and William R. Archer, of Pittsfield.

House—Anthony R. Mock, of Cambridge, Chairman; William H. Thompson and Elijah B. Sherman, of Chicago; David H. Harts, of Lincoln; Matthew H. Peters, of Watseka; Henry A. Ewing, of Bloomington: William L. Gross, of Springfield; John R. McFie of Coulterville; Jacob Wheeler, of Havana; Francis Bowen, of Sheridan; Samuel Mileham, of Camp Point; T. Duane Hinckley, of Hoyleton; Henry M. Lewis, of Berwick; Bernhart F. Weber, of Havelock and William T. McCreery, of Birmingham.

Several of the gentlemen of the House Committee held Commissions in the National Guard, and many of the Senators had promised to give the heartiest support to such Bill as should be brought forward with the recommendation of the Militia.

Upon the election of Governor Cullom, Gen. Hilliard became desirous of being re-appointed Adjutant General, and he asked Gen. Ducat's favorable services in his behalf. They were cheerfully rendered, as Gen. Hilliard had been industrious and faithful in his labors. Gen. Ducat made a personal visit to the Governor elect in November, when he presented the claims of Gen. Hilliard, and in the following month he wrote this letter:

"CHICAGO, Dec. 29th, 1876.
" HON. SHELBY M. CULLOM, Springfield, Ills.:
" *Dear Sir*,—Referring to our meeting at the Grand Pacific Hotel last November, I take the liberty of reminding you of my opinion, expressed on that occasion, of the services of Adjutant Genl. Hilliard. He has been most faithful and efficient in doing all he could, in the absence of any good military code, to organize, with the slender means at his disposal, our State

Militia, and infusing into it the proper military spirit becoming an orderly and peace-loving people.

" Though of the same politics as yourself, and a consistent, though very undemonstrative supporter of, and worker for, the Republican party, I cannot make any party claim, and would not if I could.

" I desire to simply say to you that I think the continuation of Genl. Hilliard in the office of Adjutant Genl. would be for the good of the Militia service of the State, in which I am very deeply interested, with other gentlemen of my Staff, and old military friends and officers of the State Militia.

" I shall do myself the honor and pleasure of attending upon you with my Staff on the 8th prox.

" I have the honor to be, sir,

" Very respectfully, your obt. servt.,

" ARTHUR C. DUCAT, *Brig. Genl.*"

There were many candidates for this office, and these representations of Gen. Ducat had great weight with Governor Cullom, in the selection of his Adjutant General.

Gen. Hilliard was reappointed, and he remained Adjutant General of Illinois, until the Summer of 1881, when he was succeeded by Gen. Elliott.

The Committee appointed by the Convention of officers had held three meetings only, of which the members from the First Brigade and the Division Staff had had notice; one at Chicago during the Summer, and two at Springfield, one on October 14, and the other November 20, 1878.

On this last occasion, a new Code was written, embracing all the features desired by the Militia throughout the State, and when the news was received in Chicago, that Mr. Mock, Chairman of the House Committee, had

" presented a voluminous Bill prepared by the Convention of Militia officers to draw up a Military Code," it was generally supposed of course that it was the Bill from the hands of the Committee.

The friends of the Militia however, very quickly discovered that the Code proposed by Chairman Mock was entirely different from the provisions of the Bill prepared by the Militia officers. This Code made a radical change in the command of the troops. It abolished the office of Major General, and virtually left the Adjutant General in Command, as it directed the three Brigadier Generals to report directly to him.

The office of Adjutant General is a political one. He is appointed by the Governor, and is subject to removal at the Governor's option. He is entitled to no command. He is merely the Military Secretary or Clerk of the Governor, a civil officer. His clerical duties require him to attest all military papers of State, as does the Secretary of State with civil papers, and Military Commissions and orders are sent through his office in precisely the same manner as the Commissions of Notary Public, and other civil offices are transmitted from the office of Secretary of State.

This Bill, as introduced, left the rank of the Adjutant General as Major General, and was " not only in opposition to all the principles involved in correct Military organization; but it was a dangerous accumulation of power in the hands of a politician—for such would be the position of the Adjutant General, in case this Monstrosity became a law."

As soon as the nature of this Bill became known,

there was a general protest from the Militia. The papers throughout the State exposed the measure, and the Tribune, Times and Inter Ocean, of Chicago, were united, for once, in a common cause. The vehement editorials of these papers at this time, show that there prevailed a very great indignation over the character of this proposed law, more particularly in Chicago and the other populous sections of the State.

Of course the matter was represented in its true light to individual members of the Legislature. The Citizens' Association of Chicago, which since its organization, has been constantly on the watch for the conservation and advancement of the public welfare, caused the following petition to be circulated throughout all the large Cities of the State, viz :

" *To the Members of the Legislature of the State of Illinois :*

" We, the undersigned, Citizens of the State of Illinois, have seen during the past two years the friendly and successful efforts of the Major General Commanding the Division of the Illinois National Guard, and the Brigadier Generals Commanding the Brigades, to bring the Illinois National Guard to a state of commendable efficiency.

"We understand a bill has been presented to the Legislature of the State of Illinois providing a Military Code for the State, and purporting to be a Bill from a Committee of the Officers of the Illinois National Guard, legislating out of Office the Major General Commanding the Division, and in no manner fairly representing the views of that Committee, nor those of the officers and men composing the National Guard, nor of the Citizens interested in its well being.

" That we hereby desire to remonstrate against any Bill abolishing the Office of Major General Commanding the

Division of the Illinois National Guard, and placing his authority in the Adjutant General, an officer appointed by the Governor and removable at his will, as being unmilitary and calculated to destroy the efficiency of the Illinois National Guard.

" That the introduction of any such measure looking to the aggrandizement of the Adjutant General, will result in the defeat of an improved Military Code, so much needed to secure the safety and welfare of the State.

" We therefore petition your honorable body to retain the Office of Major General Commanding the Division, and to reduce the rank of the Adjutant General from Major General to that of Colonel, and that the pay of said Officer be $1,500 per year, as we are credibly informed that Officers and gentlemen of National reputation can be found to occupy said position for that sum."

This document was signed by so large a number of the tax-paying citizens from all parts of the State, that it could not very well be ignored; and a joint-meeting of the Military Committees was held Febuary 11th, at which a Sub-Committee, consisting of two from the the Senate, Munn and Bash, and three from the House, Mock, Sherman and Harts, was appointed, to convene at the Grand Pacific Hotel in Chicago, on Monday afternoon, February 17th, to hear and consider such suggestions as might be offered by those interested in the new Militia Bill, and word was sent officially to the Division, Brigade and Regimental Headquarters of the action of the Committee.

Col. Appleton, without delay, notified all of the officers of the forces in Chicago to assemble at Division Headquarters, on February 12th; and at the time speci-

fied, all of the Chicago Commands were represented,
many interested citizens being also in attendance; and
the work of settling upon the terms of a new Bill was
taken up without delay. Meetings were held on February
12th, 13th, 14th and 15th; and at length, provisions satisfactory to all were agreed upon, and the Division Judge
Advocate was requested to draw the bill, so that it might
be ready for the Legislative Sub-Committee.

On Monday, February 17th, Messrs. Munn and Bash
of the Senate, and Mock, Sherman and Harts of the
House, received the Militia delegation in the parlor of
the Grand Pacific Hotel. There were present, Brig.
Gen. William E. Strong, Inspector General; Brig. Gen.
Samuel B. Sherer, Chief of Cavalry; Brig. Gen. Lewis
Schaffner, Paymaster General and Col. William H.
Thompson, Aide-de-Camp, of the Govenor's Staff—Brig.
Gen. J. T. Torrence of First Brigade, and Lieut. Col.
George R. Cannon, Assistant Adjutant-General; Major
John Lanigan, Assistant Inspector; Major Fernand
Henrotin, Surgeon, and Lieutenant Edward T. Sawyer,
Aide-de-Camp of his Staff—Col. E. D. Swain, Major E.
B. Knox, Major Truman W. Miller, Surgeon; Capt.
Chas. R. E. Koch, and Quartermaster John D. Bangs
of the First Regiment—Col. James Quirk, Major Peter
J. Hennessey and Adjt. John McKeough of the Second
Regiment—Major Dominick Welter and Capts. William
S. Brackett and H. H. Anderson, First Regiment of
Cavalry—Lieut. Col. Moses W. Powell and Major B. R.
DeYoung of the Sixth Battalion—Lieut. Col. John B.
Fithian of the Twelfth Battalion — Major Gen. A. C.
Ducat, and Lieut. Col. Samuel Appleton, Assistant

Adjutant-General; Lieut. Col. Jerome F. Weeks, Surgeon; Major Albert L. Coe, Quartermaster and Major Holdridge O. Collins, Division Judge Advocate, of his Staff.

A large delegation of the Citizens' Association, headed by Col. John Mason Loomis, George M. How and C. M. Henderson, was also on hand.

Col. Swain, on behalf of the officers present, made a concise statement of the position of the Militia, and presented to Senator Munn the new Bill for a law, requesting him to introduce it to the Legislature. Col. Loomis and Mr. Henderson presented the views of the Citizens' Association, and urged the committee to impress upon the Legislature the necessity of a new law, and the danger of allowing the Militia to be controlled by political leaders and party factions.

This Bill was printed at large in the Chicago papers of February 18th, with comments of hearty approval.

The Sub-Committee remained three days in Chicago. examining into the condition and wants of the Militia, and upon their return to Springfield, they reported back to the Joint Committee, recommending the adoption of this Bill, received at Chicago, and on March 5th, Mr. Munn introduced it into the Senate.

It was referred to the proper Committee, but nothing was afterwards heard of it.

The Bill in the House received a sudden impetus upon the news of a great Communistic parade in Chicago, on Sunday, April 20th, the anniversary of the Paris Commune. There were several thousand men in line, of whom twelve hundred had been uniformed, drilled and organized into Companies and Battalions. Of these, four hundred were armed with the latest and most improved model of breech-loading rifles, and their discipline and soldierly march showed that in a peaceable community, a small army had been secretly formed, composed of the worst elements of a large foreign population, whose openly expressed object was the disruption of all existing social and political institutions. They were composed principally of Bohemians, Poles and Scandinavians of the Socialist taint. Their banners were the red and black flags, and the numerous mottoes were directed more particularly against the passage of any Militia law.

" Never before, in the history of civilized communities, did 400 men, armed with breech-loading rifles and fixed bayonets, parade the peaceful streets of a great city, in order, as they express it, ' to show the Legislature and people of Chicago what they can do.' The parade was a threat. It was a threat against law, order, decency, life and property. It was a menace to the liberty which all men love—a declaration of war against all that honest men hold sacred."

Section 5, of Article XI, of the House Bill, prohibiting the drill, organization or parade of any armed body, other than the Militia, was now its principal feature. The attention of the Legislature became centered upon that clause, and losing sight of the other portions of the Bill, by an extraordinary revolution in the sentiment of the House, which was brought about by this armed Communistic demonstration in Chicago, three days afterwards, on April 23d, the Bill was passed by a vote of 100 to 37, and sent to the Senate, where it was finally passed, with a few immaterial amendments, on May 22d, by a vote of

31 to 10. The House concurred in the Senate amendments, and the Act was approved by Governor Cullom, and went into effect the following first of July, 1879.

The Legislature at this session also appropriated a liberal amount for the payment of the Militia and all expenses incurred during the riots of July, 1877.

In June, 1879, just four years from the date of his appointment as Brigadier General by Gov. Beveridge, Gen. Ducat resigned his commission as Major General, and with his Staff retired from the Military service of the State.

During the time he was in command, the greatest cordiality prevailed between himself and the officers and men of the different Regiments and Brigades. Many of them had fought with him through the campaigns of the war, and they were quick to seize upon his ideas for the organization of the Militia, and they afforded him assistance without which his labors had been futile.

The general rules for the government of the Militia, established by him, have been practically adopted in the Adjutant General's department, and their influence will be felt in the control of the troops, as long as our present system of State Militia shall exist.

To General Strong is due the credit of having inaugurated as complete an Inspection service as existed in any State of the Union; and the establishment of a regular course of rifle practice and competition for rewards, was owing entirely to that peculiar characteristic of his, denominated by Tristram Shandy as " perseverance in a good cause and obstinacy in a bad one." Although he, also, has retired, the regulations which he inaugurated are now in force, modified to suit the present form of independent Brigade Commands.

The usefulness of a well trained and reliable Militia, was practically demonstrated to the Citizens of this State, by the preservation of millions of dollars in Railroad, Mining and Manufacturing interests, and the prompt suppression of disorder in July, 1877. And Illinois, free from debt, with resources unlimited, can well afford to extend a liberal hand for the maintenance of an executive power which will always be prompt, obedient, faithful and patriotic.

SHORT Statement of what has been done for the home Military service in other States, may be of interest.

The tax of one mill, asked from our Legislature in 1877, which was reduced to one-twentieth of a mill, was based upon a comparison of the appropriations made in Massachusetts, Connecticut, New York and Pennsylvania in 1876, somewhat modified, in view of the well known difficulty in obtaining an appropriation from the Representatives of a people largely agricultural.

In Massachusetts, the number of men in active service, including officers, was 3,762, but the maximum allowed by law was 4,134. The estimates, which were approved, for 1877, based upon the maximum force, were $157,480. This sum was to be expended for pay of troops, transportation, rifle-range, pits and targets, horses, clerical hire and Headquarter expenses.

Connecticut has a force of 2,500, composing one Brigade of four Regiments, commanded by a Brigadier General. They have a regular military fund aggregating $80,000 per year, collected from those liable to military duty by a tax of $2.00 per year. In 1876, the State expended $40,000 for pay of men and officers, each at $2.00 per day when on regular duty; $19,000 for Armories, rents, care of arms, etc., and $14,000 for transportation to the Centennial Exposition, as the regular encampment of the entire Brigade took place at Philadelphia at the expense of the State. The usual expenses for transportation, at the Annual Brigade encampment amount to about $5,000. The State allows twenty-five dollars every five years to each non-commissioned officer and private for a uniform, and in addition to that, overcoats, knapsacks, blankets and equipments are provided.

Pennsylvania allowed $400 per annum for each *Company*, to be distributed among the members, and the further sum of $100 for payment of armory rent. In towns having a population exceeding 15,000, each *Company* was paid $200 for armory rent. In 1874, there were 158 Companies, to whom were paid $86,300; in 1875, there were 184 Companies to whom were paid $100,000, and in 1876, 172 Companies received $93,000.

In each of the years indicated, Companies which failed to reach the required standard for efficiency, discipline and drill, were not paid. The number of Companies limited by law was 200, and the minimum number for each Company was forty enlisted men and three Commissioned officers.

In New York the appropriations have been as follow,

viz: 1876, $275,000; 1877, $300,000; 1878, $350,000: 1879, $350,000, and since, $300,000 annually. These amounts have been paid out for the current expenses of the command. All of the larger Cities have beautiful and commodious armories, magazines and other buildings, erected by public taxation and used by the State Militia for military purposes only.

In Illinois, the following amounts have been levied and collected for military purposes since the enactment of the law of 1877:

On assessment for the year 1877,					-		$41,850 88.
"	"	"	"	"	1878,	-	-	63,694 95.
"	"	"	"	"	1879,	-		70,952 54.
"	"	"	"	"	1880,	-	-	71,280 41.
"	"	"	"	"	1881,	-		72,092 51.
"	"	"	"	"	1882,	-	-	73,173 43.

In 1883 the General Assembly appropriated for expenses of the National Guard, $75,000 per annum.

The amounts expended in Illinois have been very small compared to the appropriations of other States, while the necessities for a strong military force, owing to her geographical position, her rapidly increasing Manufacturing and Railroad interests, and the cosmopolitan character of her citizens, are certainly as great as those of any other Commonwealth of the Nation.

Illinois should have at least ten thousand men enrolled in twenty Regiments of Infantry, of which three should be at Chicago, with one full Regiment of Cavalry.

Each Regiment of Infantry should have a Gatling gun, manned by a special detail, and there should be at least four complete Batteries of three Napoleon guns each; one at Chicago, one at Quincy, one at Springfield, and one at Cairo, with an additional three inch rifled gun at Quincy and Cairo.

Spacious and convenient State Arsenals and Magazines should be erected at Chicago, Quincy, Peoria, Springfield and Cairo, with an ample provision for adequate supplies of ammunition for target practice.

There should be an intermediate sole Commander between the troops and the Adjutant General of the State, whether it be a Brigadier General commanding the entire force in one Brigade, similar to the Connecticut plan, or a Major General in charge of 'a Division with two or more Brigades, as in Pennsylvania and New York.

The entire reports from all the troops in the State should be sent to one General Commanding officer, by whom they would be duly forwarded to the Adjutant General of the State, with proper recommendations.

The present system of independent commands in Illinois lacks cohesion, and there is nothing in it to call forth any unity of feeling. There is absolutely no intercourse, officially, between the different Brigades, and the officers and men, in their military service, are as much strangers to each other as if they belonged to different States.

The most desirable form would be a Division of three or four Brigades, with the immediate, absolute command vested in a Major General, subject, of course, to the Constitutional supreme authority of the Governor, as Commander-in-Chief.

A regular, fixed tax, bringing a revenue sufficiently

large for a liberal support of the Militia, is preferable to a Biennial appropriation, which is always uncertain and unsatisfactory, as there is no surety of a stable, future provision.

The support or abolition of the State Military should rest solely upon the necessity for its use.

No questions of political supremacy, or the personal ambition and aggrandizement of individuals, should be permitted to thrust themselves forward in a deliberate consideration of this subject.

If there is no use for a Militia it should be disbanded, as any expense, however small, will be a misappropriation of the public money.

On the other hand, if the necessity for this force does exist, the wealthy and prosperous State of Illinois can well afford a liberal expenditure for the fostering care and generous maintenance of her Military children.

Finis.

www.ingramcontent.com/pod-product-compliance
Lightning Source LLC
Chambersburg PA
CBHW022343020726
47500CB00004B/1261